How to be a Smarter House Buyer
By Jon Charters-Reid

How to be a Smarter House Buyer
By Jon Charters-Reid

I'm a
SMART
House Buyer

Published in 2016 by Jonnysoundbyte Ltd

First published 2016

ISBN 978-1-5272022-0-7

Edited by Rupert Waddington,
www.texteffect.co.uk

Illustrations by The Fuse Creative Marketing Ltd
www.thefuse.co.uk

Dedication

I am dedicating this book to the highly skilled team of staff who have worked tirelessly and innovatively for me for many years. Their hard work and daily efforts have made a huge contribution, allowing this book to be published. All of our staff really do care about our customers and take a personal interest in seeing the job through from the beginning to the end. We take personal ownership of everything, and this book has been written as a result of their success!

Thank you.

How to be a smarter house buyer

Contents

Preface

House buying in the England and Wales is a massive expense and a stressful process. It is also fundamentally flawed. And so I have written this book to expose the flaws, to advise buyers on how to avoid the expensive and potentially disastrous mistakes, and to continue my campaign for fundamental change in how our housing market works.

Change has to happen, and it needs to happen quickly. In fact, six months is all it would take, a year at most, for the government to take action and fix everything that is currently wrong with the market.

The result would be a property market improved to the benefit of everyone involved - vendors, buyers and all of the professional people who are part of the process.

When my views meet resistance, it's always the same old adage - *'we've always done it this way'*. But this is irrelevant because the current system is simply not fit for purpose. The problem is that no one can be bothered to change even though the benefits from doing so will be huge.

With this book I will appear to be putting my head on the chopping block; me, a highly qualified Chartered Surveyor with a hard-earned reputation to protect.

But I don't see it that way because I am telling things the way I see them. The property market is badly structured and homebuyers need to know why and how it impacts on them.

What to expect from the book: I want to help house buyers become *smart* house buyers. So I will explain why the market is broken and faulty, and then give you some simple practical advice to help you navigate your way around the dangers and invest your money in a sound purchase and a great home.

I also offer my thoughts on how we – professionals and government – can start making changes for the better right now.

Jon Charters-Reid

BSc MRICS MCIOB MCABE

Chartered Building Surveyor

Chartered Building Engineer

RICS Registered Valuer

Contact me at ***office@uksurveys.net***

Part 1: How the housing market is broken

1. A Broken market

I firmly believe that the housing market in England and Wales is broken and that is mainly due to the activities of the corporate world. Big business and national government have both contributed to a market that is overly complex, insufficiently regulated and that fails to work on a local level.

COMPLEXITY

When you buy your house, it's not just you and the seller involved; there are the buyer's solicitor and the seller's solicitor; there's the estate agent and there's usually a bank involved too. That's at least six parties in every transaction.

But as properties often sell in chains, multiply that number by however many properties are in the chain and it becomes seriously complicated. A six-chain property might have 36 interested parties, each of them running up costs and charges. To make things even worse, not all of these will be acting as independently as you may think, something I talk about later in the book.

However, what I find even more alarming is that the whole property buying process is the wrong way round. Essentially, when you buy a house you look around it, decide you like it and you immediately engage the services of a solicitor. The solicitor is then told to get on with the purchase and the process begins in earnest. But at this stage you still don't fully appreciate what you're buying. You haven't received your survey; and it's the survey that will tell you if the property is sound, the area is sound and the price sound – and if not, the cost and lifestyle implications for you should you go ahead and buy the house.

However, there's an even bigger problem - *not all surveyors will be working in your best interests.* Some are working for other interested parties (the bank or the building society) and others are frankly not adequately qualified or sufficiently knowledgeable about the area where you're buying. So, the one piece of advice I will return to again and again throughout the book is to hire an independent surveyor – within the current danger-ridden, broken market, it is the safest and wisest thing you can do.

Buying a House? you'll need a proper SURVEY

Don't rely on the mortgage man

NOT ALL SURVEYORS ARE EQUAL

People are definitely taking more interest in the different types of survey and the information surveys provide. A smart property buyer has already realised that within the surveying industry there are a few survey reports which are nothing more than a template; the surveyor simply ticks a box and then inserts a standard clause (you can read more about this in chapter 6). Therefore, they make more money for less effort, and is the opposite of how an independent surveyor works.

Now, in theory the big firms only use properly qualified surveyors, but what really worries me is the growing number of people offering property advice without any formal qualifications. At the time of writing I could point to five such surveyors in Yorkshire who advise the general public but without any qualifications whatsoever. We get potential clients calling us to say, "ABC surveyors down the road can do it for half the price you are charging," and we have to explain that the person concerned is not a qualified or chartered surveyor. Nor are they a qualified architect or chartered engineer.

To me this is a major sign of the extent of the broken market, that people can gamble their life's work and fortune on someone who is not qualified – and can do this without even realising. This simply cannot be right and I will continue to campaign for the sake of buyers until the situation improves.

Choosing a professional to help you

I've learned to respect clients who ask me: "Jon, how did you get to where you are?"

And it's because what they're *really* asking is whether I know my stuff, what qualifications I have and how safe they can feel with my work. That person is my kind of person and I strongly advise you to ask those types of questions. It's not surprising that these are the people who then often become lifelong clients. When you find a professional you can trust, you tend to stick with them. So it's always worth looking carefully – and asking questions.

THE CORPORATE JUNGLE

I worry about the impact on the market of the big national corporate companies - estate agencies, surveyor practices, websites offering cheap surveys and the massive national corporate solicitors. To my mind, they are like a huge corporate sausage machine.

Being profit-focused, they will always look for ways to trim back what you actually get from them, but the most important factor is local knowledge; they never have as much as a truly local professional. From my own experience over the last 22 years, I find that the people who genuinely care about the property buyer are the local surveyor, the local solicitor, the local mortgage adviser and the local estate agent.

WORKING WITH BUILDERS

It doesn't matter whether you're buying a brand new house or something with a little age and history – your experience as a buyer and home-owner will be affected by builders. However, in this country we don't regulate the building profession and as a result, it is rife with unqualified and inexperienced builders.

I think the major problem is with some firms who claim to be builders but have few professional qualifications between them. Some are well intentioned but not very good; others are just cowboys, crooks who will exploit any opportunity to do shoddy work and charge through the nose.

This situation is of such grave concern that I have started an online petition to lobby the government to bring in the licensing of builders, and at the time of writing the former Mayor of London, Boris Johnston, was looking into this. It is quite simply a huge issue and something that should be addressed as soon as possible (and I have dedicated an entire chapter 7 – Defects and defective builders - exclusively to what it can mean for a home-buyer).

So, from construction to surveys, what the industry really needs is careful regulation of and by qualified property professionals. However, that alone won't fix the broken market. Let's take a quick look at the economics of the housing market, something that needs urgent attention in a world that is becoming ever more financially unstable and incapable of meeting the demand for housing.

2. *The economics of a broken market*

The economics of today's housing market have been distorted by successive governments' short-sighted policies. Looking back to Roman times no matter who was in power, there was always a long-term plan in place to develop their cities. And those plans were carried out without break. Nowadays, our governments seem incapable of developing and sustaining long term plans beyond their 5 year terms.

As a result, the biggest problem we now face is a chronic and growing housing shortage. My challenge to any government is that if you put the right professionals in charge of resolving this shortage as quickly as possible, we could do it in less than two years. It would require *carte blanche* over planning processes but it is achievable. However, for now we live with the realities of short-termist policies and the unchecked economic foundations of the broken market.

TRADITIONAL LAWS OF ECONOMICS DO NOT APPLY

Smart buyers need to understand that the traditional laws of economics do not apply in the housing market because people are still using old economic principles to it. This is true of the housing market today and, indeed, the UK's housing market over the last ten years. To my mind, the market has effectively been distorted by the appearance of buy to let investors. Also, the housing market is so broken that people wanting to move house are having to move into rented accommodation first in order to be in a stronger position for buying their next home.

Yet even with the strong demand, purchases still fall through for reasons which, along with the cash-rich buyers moving into rental properties, all help to skew the market.

Indeed, despite the growing numbers of sales and the restricted supply of properties coming to the market, the rate at which sales are failing to complete is increasing, according to a survey. The survey was published by an independent home buying firm which stated that the rate of sale collapse is running at 29%. One reason for this is the tougher lending criteria for borrowers means that some prospective buyers cannot secure a mortgage or are getting less than they thought they would. This is an issue that property solicitor Peter Gibson explains in detail later on in this book.

The firm behind the survey points to the growing problem of a lack of properties coming to market which is forcing prospective buyers to move quickly in order to secure their property. It also means potential buyers are making offers on properties which are less than ideal because they believe they will not find anything else in their price range. However, it's interesting too that the rate of chain collapsing accounts for one in five of those property sales falling through.

The constant and worrying focus of the housing shortage has a damaging secondary effect – it leads to fewer and fewer people putting their properties on the market in the belief that they won't find a property to buy. Yet in my view this is a false economy as the houses are available, even if the price is high.

Certainly, in the north of England most houses that go on the market in most communities sell fairly quickly. But where potential sellers sit tight, there is a shortage of supply, so the strong demand leads to rapid price increases and stronger competition among buyers to snap up those properties that do become available. Even the housing shortage that we saw during the recession distorted house prices.

SO WHY ARE WE NOT BUILDING MORE HOUSES?

You'd think with the negative political publicity caused by the problem of a housing shortage that this challenge would have been resolved by now. But we cannot physically build houses fast enough to get them onto the market. The problem relates to our building industry (and I touch on this again in chapter 7) and our overstretched local authorities that lack enough staff to deal with planning applications and the enforcing of building regulations.

Across England and Wales house prices are not in a state of constant price rocketing. However, when discussing the housing market it is important to remember that London and some parts of the South of England have very different experiences. London is the house price capital of the world. What has been happening in London with property prices growing so strongly bears no shape or resemblance to the housing market outside of the capital.

It is no understatement when I say that the housing market is being hoisted by its own petard, and this lack of building new homes is the fundamental problem. In essence, the property market is now caught in a cycle with: a) some people moving from their house into a rented house which is not on the market in order for them to buy a house that is going to come onto the market; b) people renting because there are not enough affordable homes on the market; and c) simply not enough property within the UK's housing market for sale.

If this situation was not bad enough, we have also had a population explosion with people from other European Union countries looking to enjoy better employment prospects and lots of vulnerable refugees looking for somewhere safe to live. And within the existing population, when the figures are analysed it becomes clear that the UK has seen a big growth in the number of single person households and divorced families needing more than one property. Also as any university town knows, there has been massive growth in student houses to meet the expanding student market.

We need to stop this pain and act radically to boost the number of properties available. I have said this before and I will say it again; after World War II we managed to create a huge explosion in the number of properties available by undertaking a massive house-building project. Now we are seeing governments of whatever hue simply not acting in a way that will resolve the problem. My suggestion to put the right professionals in charge of the situation would see new houses built more quickly; and it would have little or no impact on prices and thereby have no adverse impact on existing owners' investments.

THE IMPACT OF INTEREST RATES

At the time of writing, no one is quite sure when the predicted rise in interest rates will actually take place. Homeowners have been living for years with the possibility that interest rates will have to rise but the increase never happens. Meanwhile, the Governor of the Bank of England continues to predict a stepped rise over a set period of time. All of this simply fuels anxiety and uncertainty in the market, creating a huge disincentive to trade up or take that first step onto the property ladder.

By merely *signalling* the possibility of a rise in interest rates, people's – and lenders' – perceptions change, resulting in an increase in mortgage rates and a slowing of the housing market. It would be so much better if the Bank of England gave us clearer intentions of future interest rates.

For those of us who watch these developments closely, we have noticed a change in the language being used. For instance, when the Bank began saying that interest rates 'might' be going up, everyone took a sharp intake of breath. Then people said that yes, interest rates must go up because savings are being eroded as the cost of living overtakes interest rate returns. Certainly, when interest rates do rise there will inevitably be an impact on people's financial outgoings as their mortgage repayments increase.

I do believe that the Bank of England is testing the waters to see what people's reactions would be to a rise, effectively to see what they can get away with. So the Bank push up the base interest rate by 0.5% (or even 0.25%) just to see how the markets react. I think the Bank is taking a preparatory step by making statements to test the potential reactions to an actual increase in the base rate. The big question is whether the Bank will follow in the footsteps of the US Federal Reserve that has raised interest rates, or whether it will retain these historically low rates whilst there is volatility in the global economy.

What about negative interest rates?

There is a theory that negative interest rates lead to reduced mortgage rates, and some potential buyers may be waiting for this to happen. However, it seems very unlikely that the Bank would ever opt for negative interest rates as this might lead to a lack of control over monetary policy and would create instability in the financial sector as banks would not know where to hold their money. Were negative interest rates to be introduced, banks would respond by buying very liquid government bonds in order to avoid the negative charges on balance sheets.

Therefore, it seems highly unlikely that the prospective buyer can sit around waiting for further interest rate falls in the future, which would make their potential mortgages cheaper.

A DIFFERENT FINANCIAL MODEL?

'I have a 1974 car, and I have all the tools I need in my garage to keep it running well.'

For the buyer of a *modern* car, however, the best traditional toolkit in the world will be of little use. It's a new technology. And the same mismatch exists in the world economy.

You see, from the viewpoint of the property market, the one major thing that's wrong with our economy is that the commentators and policy makers are still using an old method to calculate its health. Global finances are managed through brand-new technology, and today's post-recession world bears little resemblance to its pre-recession forebear.

So, even if this causes a few raised eyebrows, I suggest that we need to ditch the old ways, stop using e=mc2 and start promoting a flowering of new thinking.

For example, we have seen the enormous impacts of credit downgrading on some countries and organisations, but at the same time this has little or no impact on a financial world where billions of Dollars, Pounds and the Yen are moved instantly every day.

The world of finance has moved on, and I believe we now need an international web-based balance sheet to keep track of this money and its impact on world economies rather than looking at individual organisations and countries.

My other worry is that the stock market is run by 'bulls' and only looks five or ten minutes ahead in what is basically a reactive process. So while there are some long-term investment opportunities in the stock market, world economics are influenced by short-term gain and a reactive perspective.

Again, someone needs to come along with a new form of thinking and assessment so that we can effectively monitor and measure economic prosperity and performance, giving us a truer indication of what is going on financially and enabling better forward planning.

This is precisely why we are seeing so much volatility in the Chinese economy as no-one has a clue about the value of firms on the stock market there.

New thinking really can help transform the housing market:

We are already seeing parents taking equity from their home to help their children get onto the housing ladder. I can foresee a time when banks and building societies begin offering a lifetime or a generational mortgage rather than the traditional one that lasts up to 25 years. This would enable much more flexible financial management across successive generations, and already happens in some European countries.

The diagram on the next page illustrates joined-up thinking achieved by all parties collaborating to develop a Super Plan for the economy:

My 'Super plan' for the economy. Note: CML is for Council of Mortgage Lenders.

3. *Impact of the Buy to Let culture*

I want house buying (and selling) to be easier than it is right now – so you might think I'm against the buy to let market? Well, I'm not. Buy to let offers a sensible income and investment option for people. However, it takes prospective new homes off the market – and for as long as we are not replacing these homes with new properties for home-buyers, I do not champion the growth in buy to let. But it's what we live with right now, and it has skewed the market for first-time buyers and others, so putting it right means understanding why it grew so fast in the first place.

Buy to let is a market – it responds to market forces and, as such, it reflects the rise in demand for rental property amongst people who cannot afford to buy. However, one reason for this is that they believe they cannot get a mortgage, and to my mind this is simply not true. In many cases, if you look at how much people are paying in rent and how much they would pay in mortgage repayments, they would save money by buying a property. There is an issue about saving the money for a deposit and there are a growing number of 95% mortgages available (with unfavourable interest rates).

So here is another opportunity for fresh thinking. The banks need to find an innovative way to meet the untapped demand for mortgages. It's a great opportunity for them as they would see a growth in the number of people signing up for bank accounts, life assurance and pensions as well as other products such as car loans and credit cards. Despite the push for easy bank switching, banks can still expect to get a sizeable proportion of customers for life, so this is a lucrative opportunity that is being missed.

We also need to understand why people were rushing into buy to let as a worthwhile investment and this is partly down to the actions of successive governments. Lots of people have seen their pension fall in value over time and are looking to make a sound investment for their retirement. We can't blame investors since various governments have taken money out of peoples' pensions and savers are faced with poor interest rates. In the search for other asset classes, the strong performance of property in recent years makes it a natural choice.

The new buy to let changes though still worthwhile are aimed at cooling the market down – though many 'amateur' landlords will find themselves struggling to make a profit from the changes to stamp duty, how much they can claim in expenses and the fact they will have to pay tax on turnover and not profit. Some buy to let experts are predicting that by 2020 many landlords with one or two properties will have left the sector altogether as they increasingly find buy to let properties unprofitable.

When we are discussing the buy to let market we should also appreciate that the work of social housing providers goes unacknowledged and it's greatly underfunded. They do amazing work and they could do with more money. At present they simply cannot meet demand, so this leaves an exploitable gap in the market for private landlords.

There's also another issue concerning 'self-certification mortgages', better known in the industry as 'liar mortgages'. These products enabled someone to declare their income for borrowing purposes without that income being independently verified. Looking back, I almost wish I had taken advantage of these products to acquire more property, but I felt they were morally wrong. However, I know of landlords who used them to buy 10 or even 20 properties without their financial stability being checked in any way. The banks were effectively taking a huge gamble on the massive roulette wheel of housing and the bet paid off because the properties rose quickly in value; everyone was, for a time, a winner.

Another driver in the growth of this market has been a lack of good policy to help people plan financially for their retirement, especially in the long period of low interest rates. With a lack of options for securing an income in old age, many investors looking around anxiously for future security opted for property investment.

As a result, people are using buy to let in lieu of an adequate pension. And the property market has delivered rewards in capital growth.

Once again, I'm not blaming people for trying to protect their money; in my view the government has failed to monitor and manage the housing and other issues properly. Without mentioning any names, I met with someone offering to help the government resolve the pension crisis. The government looked at his proposal and said it was a brilliant idea but could not be implemented. Why? Because they could only operate on a five-year basis and his idea would take longer than that.

How to be a smarter house buyer

4. The pressure cooker syndrome

There are many reasons why selling a house and completing a sale is nothing short of a miracle in this day and age. Indeed, it is a

miracle that such a complicated system has ever actually worked and someone has managed to move; and let's not forget that a lot of sales fall through – even on the day the contracts are due to be exchanged.

Part 3 of this book contains tips and advice for being a smart house buyer. And perhaps the most important of these is to do the right research, to do your homework first. Homework means turning detective and looking beyond just the property itself. However, stepping into the housing market is like being inside a pressure cooker. The one thing you never feel able to do is to take your time – and without that, you will make bad decisions.

Visit any electrical appliance shop and you will see couples spending ages looking at the goods; whether it's a washing machine, fridge or even a toaster they have, in all probability, already been on the internet and know what the products are and what they cost and which is the best one to buy within their price range. They have done their homework and do not want to be sold something that will later let them down.

However, when it comes to the same people buying a house, I can tell you that they will probably walk through the doorway and immediately fall in love with the property. Lots of people will buy a home with their heart rather than with their head. I am not kidding when I tell people that there are lots of homebuyers who get no further than the front door or hall before deciding they will buy the property. People even spend longer test-driving a potential new car than they do examining every aspect of a house they're considering.

Indeed, it isn't just me saying this, a survey from a conveyancing services firm has revealed that Britain is a nation of decisive homebuyers who fall in love with a property and act quickly to buy it. Alongside facts that nearly two in three homeowners were able to buy the home they originally fell in love with - and 25% were lucky enough for this to be the first property debuted - an impressive 18% made a decision to buy their home within 30 seconds of entering the property! That's 30 seconds! The research also points out that 26% made a decision to buy before they had viewed the whole property. It is a serious point I'm making when I claim that most homebuyers today will spend more time deciding on which type of car or vacuum to buy than they will on buying their home.

I help buyers to step back and see the bigger picture. For example, I went to a house in a coastal town with some smart buyers and I spent all day long at that property with them. In addition, we also walked up and down the street to see what the neighbouring houses were like and we even got in my car to drive around the surrounding area to see if there were any potential problems. We examined every aspect of that purchase and I even told the couple that they should return to the property at night to see whether there were any unforeseen problems that were not apparent during the daytime.

Another pressure point occurs when the buyer is simultaneously going through the process of selling their own home, and so the pressure doubles with the clock running fast. This means the buyer has to make quick decisions and move quickly on a property they want to buy. This is why estate agents in areas where house buying is a fierce competition are urging buyers to sell their property first and then move into rental property.

This then puts them in a stronger position to buy because they will not be in a chain with the risks of it breaking. It makes them a more attractive buyer. And whilst the pressure is so great, this is good advice that I agree with.

There are some very strange stories behind sales falling through...

Recently we had a client about to complete on a house; out of the blue the vendors received a phone call from the estate agent saying that the couple had fallen out and they no longer wanted to buy the property. The woman in the relationship called the estate agent to ask what was going on; the agent was surprised but expressed her sympathy about the failed relationship. Unfortunately, while her partner had indeed decided it was over, he had not actually bothered to tell his partner this fact.

Let's be honest, with so many variables and such a complex variety of people involved within every transaction, it cannot come as a surprise that so many sales do not complete when the pressure of time is added to the mix. For anyone who needs a mortgage, the lender is interested in getting that application through as quickly as possible, which speeds up the entire process. Where there is a scarcity of property for sale, people are over-keen on making a bid and buying the property quickly. This means that there is a race between buyers to get a bid in and snap up the property.

There are places in the world where it's possible to buy a house within two weeks but that's because they have a much simpler and more efficient system. It should be possible in England and Wales to follow a simpler process and in a more controlled manner. Without the pressure, a house buyer will be able to make a reasoned and careful judgement on the property they want to buy. However, the pressure of so many elements coming together, and with each looking out for its own interests, can force the wrong kind of quick decision.

I honestly believe that buying a property in England and Wales in the 21st-century is far more complicated process than it needs to be. We can make the process easier but the will to do so does not appear to be there. And I find this baffling because everyone involved in selling and buying homes will benefit from a more effective process. Ask any estate agent in the country how many transactions fall through at the last minute and they will say they have a substantial number. As surveyors, we see an element of these 'fall throughs' ourselves when clients come back to us and say they didn't buy the property after all because of details in our report that they had missed when they visited the house.

I just want to end this part of the book by stressing that although my mission is to highlight the benefits of using a good, independent surveyor, I also want to stand up for local hard working estate agents around the country – and chapter 12 is dedicated to the topic. Many people malign it as a profession and there is simply too much estate agent bashing going on.

Being an estate agent is not an easy job to do. I have been in lots of estate agents' offices over the years and I've worked for a couple of estate agents as well and they really do work hard for their money. Critics say that they charge a large fee for what they do but most people have no idea just how much work an estate agent will put in to sell a property.

Part 2: The challenges of buying a house

Buying a property is for most people the biggest financial risk they will ever take and yet the vast majority of those people are starting the process blind. However, it is not through ignorance; quite the reverse. These people *do* go out of their way to seek advice. And, just as you would trust your accountant or your doctor, they trust what they are told. The problem is that this advice often comes from an unreliable and/or unqualified source.

On the flipside, and in part influenced by the recent recession, we do at least now have a new type of buyer, the 'smart buyer'. The economic downturn has made some people much more cautious and demanding of the right information when making a huge decision. But the fact remains that finding this reliable information is still a challenge thanks to the current state of the market and the people that 'run' it. So in this section we'll just consider the process of buying a house and with it the different stages at which you can be exploited or misled.

5. Bank mortgages and surveys

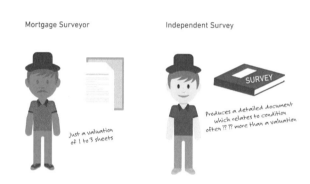

Mortgage Surveyor

Just a valuation of 1 to 3 sheets

Independent Survey

SURVEY

Produces a detailed document which relates to condition often ?? ?? more than a valuation

MORTGAGES

Which is the biggest risk – buying the wrong property or choosing the wrong mortgage to pay for it? It's a tough question to answer, but at least if the property prices fluctuate everyone is in the same boat; most properties will gain or lose roughly the same amount proportionately. This is not true

45

of fluctuations in repayment rates and the benefits or penalties attached to different individual mortgages. The problem with the current market is that you do not automatically get objective and complete advice or information.

The smart buyer of *anything* seeks independent advice; they never just accept what the seller/promoter/advertiser/agent tells them. So why is it that buyers are encouraged to approach a bank for a mortgage when the one thing this will not give them is independent advice about the full range of financial products available to them on the wider market? Banks are allowed to promote their own products without any attempt at clarifying the 'whole of market' situation. I find this incredible given the enormous financial investment being made.

Remember, an Independent Financial Advisor can offer you products from the whole of the mortgage market.

My other worry is that I have seen people go to a high street bank and be turned down for a mortgage only to be awarded exactly the same mortgage when they apply via an independent financial adviser. One reason for this is that the banks are employing young people, often extremely young and inexperienced people, who are barely school-leavers, who have not been trained correctly and who are not aware of the house buying process or even have experience of it. Unfortunately, the people who suffer are those who don't understand that you can apply for a mortgage through an Independent Financial Advisor.

So, to be a smart buyer, *always* consider consulting an independent financial adviser who will look at the entire mortgage market and find the most suitable product for you. It's well worth the effort - and remember to use one who is well-established locally too.

SURVEYS

The other area where banks are less than completely honest concerns the house survey. They muddy the water about who is and who isn't acceptable to conduct the survey. I am not saying that this is deliberate malpractice but the impact on buyers can definitely be serious as it is frighteningly easy to raise a mortgage and buy a house on the back of an inadequate survey (see chapter 8).

Banks often have their own selection of 'approved' surveyors, and they will encourage the buyer to use one of these. Some then keep a large portion of the survey fee that you pay, so their motive is clearly one of profit. However, by 'approved' they actually mean that they have a business association with those particular surveyors; they do not mean that you are not allowed to appoint your own qualified independent surveyor. Remember - the banks cannot legally tell you who and who may not do your survey, and choosing your own surveyor is exactly what you can and should do.

On a majority of Surveys carried out by the bank there is no inspection of the loft or roof void and the roof make sup at least a third of the structure of the property. Another reason to choose your own independent surveyor, remember you are a **Smarter house buyer.**

The same thing can happen when you are choosing a solicitor to do your conveyancing. Banks have been known to tell you that you must use one of their approved solicitors, but there is no law or regulation governing this. You are entitled to appoint whom so ever you like (and indeed, you can do your own conveyancing if you wish). In some parts of the country, some law firms are starting to bite back at the banks.

I know it happens – it happens to me!

I frequently get a new client coming back to me in distress having been told by their bank that they cannot after all use me as their surveyor because "I am not approved." The buyer understands this to mean that I am not sufficiently qualified. Yet not only am I as qualified as the bank's 'own' surveyors, being a member of the Royal Institute of Chartered Surveyors, I am probably considerably more qualified as I am also a chartered engineer and a chartered building surveyor. So that word "approved" is mischievously misleading and I recommend any house buyer to challenge the bank when it is used.

THE NEXT PPI SCANDAL?

We've all heard of the PPI scandal – insurance products mis-sold, for which the sellers are now paying back billions of pounds. Well, I think there may be another scandal brewing.

The problem is that if you accept the bank's surveyor, the bank will prefer to charge you by adding the fee (say £500) to the mortgage. Then, depending on your mortgage's interest rate, you can then end up paying back between £3,800 and £5,000. That's an extraordinary amount of money to pay for a survey.

What the bank should be doing is spelling out the cost of the survey as a separate unit, one that you can easily choose to pay for up front. Instead, I deem them guilty of mis-selling a product in exactly the same way as they did with insurance. It is fundamentally wrong. If the fee you pay is added to the term of the mortgage you should be provided with an illustration of how much you pay back. As it is, it's really a loan but they don't make this clear to you and it just needs a smart law firm to take the banks to task and start a new compensation claim that will stretch back years.

There is no English law to state the bank can stipulate which chartered surveyor to use. The Council of Mortgage lenders clearly state a surveyor who carries out a mortgage valuation must be a member of the " Royal Institution of Chartered Surveyors." There is no mention of an approved panel. Furthermore the bank is asking you to use a surveyor whom they have a cosy arrangement with usually by significantly increasing the fees much higher than an independent surveyor would charge. Additionally the bank keep quite a large percentage of the fee that you pay over to them.. This arrangement is with large national surveying companies. **Smarter house buyers** – will ask their bank to specify the arrangement and commission they keep with these companies.

They must give you a legal reason why you cannot use your own surveyor for the mortgage valuation. It is also a fact that you can use your own Chartered Surveyor to carry out your independent survey. This is considered conditional selling and is not treating customers fairly. A **Smarter house buyer** must challenge the bank on this every time.

6. Not all surveys are equal

This whole book is about the benefits of getting the right kind of independent advice – from people who have *your* best interests at heart and *no other interest* that might compete. Clearly, a bank trying to upsell other products is going to make more money out of you – so their interest is not the same as yours. Now, as I said, people are beginning to get wise to this and become smart buyers. But there is still a fundamental problem – and one that banks are helping to perpetuate by promoting their own 'approved' surveyors; *not all surveys are equal – but not everyone will tell you that.*

Given the size of your investment, wouldn't you think it sensible to seek the best possible advice before committing yourself? The trouble is that even if you try to find the best, there are people from within the surveying industry who don't know the difference between a survey and a property valuation. Many times I have heard bank staff call a valuation a survey and *vice versa*.

So, I will tell you and then you can make an informed decision. And making the right decision is crucial to negotiating the right price – or being smart.

To put it in a nutshell (and you can find more detailed explanations in chapter 8), a valuation is a certificate of lending to say that your house is worth, for example, £500,000. And given that this type of report (often 1 – 3 pages) is cheaper, it's no surprise that some buyers opt for it. However, banks can make a healthy profit by charging a fee for this that is closer to that of a proper survey, a reason why some surveyors refuse to work for banks. But with just a simple valuation report, you're buying a property that has not been inspected thoroughly; you're buying blind. By contrast, a survey is an in-depth report that will detail the condition of the property. And there are different levels of survey available, depending on how deep you need to probe into the condition of the property. But, of course, how can you tell how deep you need to probe except by having a proper survey?

There is also the problem of litigation. There is no doubt that legal issues have become a massive problem within the industry in recent years and the result is that companies and surveyors are compelled to couch their reports in safe terminology to avoid any potential future lawsuit. Clearly the less detailed the report, the more this fudging becomes necessary. This is something that needs to change; surveyors need greater protection from this if they are to be able to do their work properly on behalf of their client.

ALWAYS GET A SURVEY – AND DO THIS *FIRST*

When you read the section about builders and building defects, you will begin to realise that it is almost impossible to buy a house that doesn't have some kind of problem. But most problems can be fixed if identified in the first place – and at a price. And knowing that price *before* you put in your offer makes far more sense than the usual process of making an offer and then getting everyone busily involved in pushing towards completion, only for you to stall everyone by raising the subject of repairs and trying to renegotiate the price.

Remember: Condition affects Price

Paying for an independent survey will pay dividends should the report reveal serious issues with the property. However, adjusting your offer to reflect necessary repairs isn't straightforward – should a property worth £200,000 need £50,000 of remedial work carrying out then it doesn't automatically follow that you can expect to get £50,000 off the asking price. There's a reason why surveyors study at university and then spend a long time following more experienced surveyors in the field to get an appreciation of valuing properties; it is a complicated process.

This is why we should celebrate the smaller independent estate agents. I get fed-up with people talking down estate agents – they are not all the same! And over the years I have worked very harmoniously with local agents when needing to re-negotiate the price; in my view the local estate agent often has a healthy commercial focus. The independents are much more likely to work really hard for their clients; so if there's a problem, they will want to help resolve it. These independents are used to dealing with detailed survey reports and then negotiating between the vendor and buyer on a new price if an issue is highlighted within that report. If you want to lose thousands of pounds on the sale of your house use an on-line estate agent; otherwise use a local one.

Just to underline my point, here are nine great reasons why Smart Buyers and sellers should use local estate agents:

- They have the local experience that will benefit both the seller and buyer

- They will know how to market a property effectively - most will have a database of buyers waiting for a property

- Good estate agents help the selling process to enable a successful sale

- The local estate agent will offer a personal service and be approachable and friendly

- Unlike many online estate agents, the seller and buyer will know how to get hold of their estate agent because they will have an office that can be reached

• The estate agent will use their experience and expertise to get the best possible price for the property and ensure both parties are happy with the transaction

• If there are any issues such as legal problems or someone not understanding the terms being used, then the estate agent can explain them succinctly

• Good estate agents are members of an accredited body and, as such, they must abide by professional standards

• Finally, local estate agents who have been recommended have a good reputation for being good at what they do for a reason - the help people buy the home of their dreams and they help sellers find buyers. What more could a Smart Buyer want?

Don't think of surveys as making things complicated

A good survey makes your life a whole lot simpler. When inspecting a property, a surveyor is asking a simple question: is the property defective in any way? And the answer often boils down to a simple 'yes' or 'no'. If the answer is 'yes' then the surveyor can help you to decide whether the property is over-priced; and if it is, the surveyor can help you and the estate agent to find a way of revising the price to reflect the work required. Simple – and certainly much simpler than finding out *after* buying the house that you need another £20,000 - £30,000 for hidden repairs. Remember, you can ask a good surveyor any question about the property you are buying.

My final word at this point to any would-be smart buyer is this; don't be seduced by the lowest possible survey cost. I have always believed that you get what you pay for in this world.

If you cut corners on fees, you'll only face double or more in unexpected bills to put the job right.

7. Defects and defective builders

In some ways this chapter is the heart of the book. In it I combine my own commentary on the state of our building industry with some thoughts about putting things right; and with this information you, the house buyer, will know what sort of questions to ask - and *who* to ask.

It all relates to building defects.

*

Surveying is about assessing a property's strengths and weaknesses – and that means looking for defects. However, simply pointing these out isn't very helpful. What you really need to know is how serious they are and, more to the point, how difficult or expensive they will be to put right.

You might think, therefore, that surveying is all about *older* properties – and not something that concerns the buyer of a new-build. You'd be wrong. People have rose-tinted expectations of a brand new house; and, in fact, you can find some serious defects lurking in many a new building while older ones have more predictable issues that we've learned long ago how to put right.

Now, before launching in let me clarify something. I am not waging any kind of campaign against builders as a profession. We need great builders, period. But I am, as you will read, deeply concerned by the part that unscrupulous builders and the unregulated industry play in many a horror story that I hear or encounter in my work helping people to buy good houses.

WHAT IS A BUILDING DEFECT?

Most people would say that it's something wrong with the house, or something that's not working perfectly. But the question we should also be asking is *why* is it not working perfectly? And the answer is, at least for 99% of the time, 'human error' and not some defect that is already inherent in the design or materials.

As an example, imagine a pair of semi-detached houses, the type where both homes share a single continuous roof. They have obviously been built at the same time and using the same materials but each house will have its own list of individual defects; these are down to the variances that occur during the building process and to simple human error – namely builders and poor DIY.

There are of course some inherent defects, design flaws such as the classic 1930s house with an archway over a recessed front entrance porch. This archway will, in time, crack in the middle or off centre, and the most common reason for this is that the small wall on the end of the house needs to be wider to cope with the distribution of weight more effectively. The other frequent causes relate not to design flaws but to human error: the most common is when the drainpipe running alongside has never been correctly connected; others include settlement of the foundations on that corner of the house which are not as good as they should be, or because the archway has not been correctly built in the first place. The full list of possible causes is endless.

I reckon that every house design has some inherent flaws. I can take people to various types of houses and stand outside to point out what the potential problems are likely to be. Indeed, I can take someone to a row of houses and point out where the roof tiles have blown off from each property in exactly the same place because the roofs all share the same design flaw.

DEFECTS IN NEW BUILD PROPERTIES

I believe strongly that no-one has ever really considered how we build new homes in this country, and we are not being innovative enough with house design. My own firm is finding as many defects on new homes as we do on much older properties that might be 100 years old.

When I was much younger I served my time earning money on a building site, and also working as a classically-trained carpenter/joiner, all of which gave me valuable experience in property building. However, I very quickly moved away from that market because, even back then, I was not particularly impressed. I remember the term 'house bashing' being used because the builders were rushing to get the properties built. I've also worked as a site manager and some of the things I have seen over the years during the house building process are just horrific. I was a tough manager, and many who started under me soon left or were sacked; for the most part they were simply chancers, not skilled tradesmen. Only the skilled remained.

The real problem afflicting the building industry today is that volume builders are just that; they want to build houses in volume (and often as small as possible) which means working as quickly and as cheaply as possible, with little care about the product they are offering to the house buying public – they could just as easily be building rabbit hutches.

Over the years I have put together a rogue's gallery of photographs taken in newly-built properties with defects that would literally make your eyes pop-out in surprise. Among these are builders building a house brick wall out of plumb even though it can plainly be seen with the naked eye.

I've also seen new homes being built without a damp proof course, drains being attached at the wrong sloping angle so they will not drain water from the property, boiler flues being in the wrong place, kitchen doors being put on upside down, creaking floorboards, half inch gaps between stair strings and walls - loads of things that should never happen but do.

I have also been to new homes where there has been no insulation fitted even though, under building control regulations, this needs to be signed off. And I remember visiting a site where the developers had only just managed to sneak planning permission through; they had squeezed in two additional houses that were so tiny the builder had tiled around the bathroom door when it is closed because it would not open fully for the wall to be tiled properly.

I've also lost count of the number of homes that have copious amounts of rubbish under the floorboards. I've seen nails put through gas pipes and I have reported more defects in modern houses where the floor is out of level than I would care to mention. Believe it or not, the current standards allow for a tolerance for the floor being out of level – but why? It can't be asking too much to have accurate work. When the ancient Egyptians built the pyramids they were perfectly level because they used a spirit level. So why do our modern houses need a floor tolerance? It is absolute nonsense.

If you're going round a new show home, bear this in mind...

In new show houses:

- They often remove the doors to create flow
- The furniture is often smaller than normal
- Decoration is carefully chosen to enhance the space and make it look bigger
- There is always exceptional pressure on the buyer to complete

So, view the house with the right mindset. Try to imagine what the house looks like when the whole family is in it - or even better take them round with you. And try to park your car in the garage to see if fits. We are still building garages on the old British standard car size and not the new global size of car; if you can fit your car in to the garage can you actually open or close the doors?

OUR BUILDING INDUSTRY IS SIMPLY NOT GOOD ENOUGH

The English house used to have a reputation for being amongst the best-built houses in the world. We are now starting to lose not only that reputation but also the skills that led to it. From an employer's point of view it is becoming increasingly difficult to acquire and train apprentices. The building industry is stifled with health and safety rules and irrelevant regulations. And some builders are not builders at all but criminals out to play the system in my opinion.

Let me explain what I mean. About 20 years ago one of my children needed a very delicate operation on his mouth to correct a lisp. I went to the hospital and was introduced to the surgeon who was to carry out the operation. He did not look very old so I asked him, "How many of these have you done?" He replied that he had done only one but had "watched quite a few".

My response was to say very firmly that he was not going to operate on my child. And in the end we got a very experienced children's surgeon to carry out the operation. My child now speaks without a lisp and of course we are very grateful for the work that was done.

In a similar vein, houses cost many thousands of pounds and we spend all of our lives trying to buy them; it's the ambitious dream of the vast majority of people in this country to own their own home. Given this, why do we take at face value that the builder of our dream home is professionally capable of building it? In my experience many are not.

The truth is that our unlicensed building industry has been struggling; for years there has been insufficient intake of apprentices and training. And where there *is* training, it is much briefer than it used to be. In the 1980s it took three to four years for an apprentice bricklayer, plumber, electrician, roofer or joiner to be trained and qualified. That's no longer the case;

developers use employees as unit-fitting machines, not people needing to be taught real skills. Building designers are becoming less imaginative too.

However, it's not just the big building firms that are at fault, according to the Federation of Master Builders (FMB) who say that one in three small construction firms are being put off from taking on apprentices because of the bureaucracy involved. Apparently, 94% of construction firms want to train apprentices but a third are being turned off by a number of factors including the cost of employing and training an apprentice as well as the complexity of the apprenticeship process.

Simply having the word 'builder' on the side of your van does not make you a builder.

I had a client who came to me saying that she was to have a £20,000 extension built. She had already paid her builder £14,000 but he had not actually started any work. She wanted to know if this was acceptable. After a period of silent disbelief I replied that it was not.

I explained first of all that a good builder will not ask for money up front, and I then asked why she had confidence in this builder. "He has a smart sign on his van saying 'builder', and he lives in our village," was her answer. So I then told her to ask the builder whether he had served the normal apprenticeship as a bricklayer and whether he was a qualified roofer – and if not, what his particular trade actually was. She went away and asked him these questions, and then came back to me; "He has not got a trade Jon, but I've got my money back off him."

Be aware of unqualified and ill-informed builders

UNQUALIFIED AND ILL-INFORMED BUILDERS

There are lots of people working in the building trade who describe themselves as builders but have no qualifications. Electricians, plumbers and gas engineers have to be qualified, so why not builders? To my mind we have a serious issue of the 'blind leading the blind' in the building industry. This is one reason why I have an online petition urging for legislation to license builders and for them to be qualified. Sign the petition now – go to:

https://www.change.org/p/jon-charters-reid-regulation-on-builders

Take roofing; it's pretty obvious that tiles and slates should be attached in the correct way. I visited a client who had contacted me to say that he had a roofer on the job but things did not appear 'to be going right'. I got there and saw immediately that the roofer was putting the roof slates on incorrectly. I asked the roofer, "Who showed you how to fit slates like that? Who taught you to do that?" The man replied, "Well, it was Pete, the man I'm working with." Pete, who it later turned out, was a carpet fitter, then appeared and I said to him, "Pete, I'm not being funny but why have you fitted slates in this way?" He replied, "Well that's the way you do it." I asked him who had told him to do it that way and it turned out that someone else had told him to do it that way.

Well, I'm all for passing on skills through the generations, but building a house using hearsay or rumours is simply not good enough! And there's no excuse when the guidelines are there, loud and clear for any builder to follow. For example, there is a particular defect on internal roof valleys that occurs simply because around 90% of the time they have been finished incorrectly. Yet there are the NHBC (National House Building Council) guidelines that include the clearest of drawings that could be understood by a three-year-old child.

This problem of ignoring the expert guidelines is rife. And it's made worse by the general public who are misled into trusting what builders tell them. If they only knew!

I go to houses and again and again I see many things done incorrectly, standard things like a damp proof course. An example that would be funny unless it happened to you is the classic case of the septic tank. There is a ridiculous myth about throwing a dead animal into a tank to get the biological side of things going. All that it actually does is to clog up the drain with bones. But I have been on site when workers have wanted to throw a dead chicken into a tank; their work is based on this kind of nonsense, and it takes a lot of effort to convince them that it's wrong. But it doesn't stop at dead poultry…

Septic tanks also have a pipe called a 'dip pipe'. Clearly it is there for a purpose. However, I once met a man who worked for a certain local authority and we were looking at a drain and he said to me, "We always smash the dip pipe off the septic tank because it doesn't do anything." I then had to explain to him that if he looked into the British Standards for septic tanks (BS6297 if you are interested) it clearly shows that particular pipe as an integral part of the standard septic tank. So even if the builders don't understand what it's for (although they should), why aren't they referring to the correct guidelines, instead of relying on stupid advice that is passed around from builder to builder? Maybe they believe that ignorance is bliss!

So why don't we insist on builders being licensed?

Let me pose this question: how many times do you hear of a gas fitter or a registered electrician doing something wrong? Hardly ever if at all, I bet, because they are licensed and trained professionals. In the city where I live, I frequently see an electrician driving around who has been an electrician all of his life and he does everything right; I have been to houses and he puts his sticker on the meters to show that he has done the work. Even the lads who work for him have been trained correctly and his business is the perfect example, to me at least, of how things should be done.

If we licensed our builders, I believe that the quality of work done would be vastly improved. So I find the question of defects in buildings, particularly new homes, very annoying when, with a few simple steps, we could eradicate a great number of them. And it should annoy house buyers and all the

81

professional experts helping them that they work their fingers to the bone in a bid to buy a property only to find that the condition simply is not good enough. In my view many new homes are simply poorly built – you are being conned! Get a survey on a new house.

Do you get foul smells from your 1980s pipework?

It's a common problem with modern houses – but back in the 1930s it wasn't. You see, back then the soil and vent pipes had an independent run to the bath and an independent run from the sink and to the back of the toilet. However, since the 1980s builders/developers tend to connect all three of these into the one pipe. When asked why, the reply is often "because it's always been done that way". Not in the 1930s it wasn't! But too many builders are not trained properly, so they don't know.

BEWARE THE COWBOYS AND CONMEN

There is another human element to the problem of defects – deliberate deception. People are being hoodwinked and misled when buying houses, both by having serious defects disguised and by being persuaded to part with large sums for unnecessary work. Welcome to the dark world of the unscrupulous cowboys and conmen. It's not pretty, and it will convince you only ever to employ skilled tradespeople.

Some are simply anxious to play down the severity of a problem, perhaps because they don't fully understand it or how to rectify it. For instance, you could have a tiny leak from underneath the shower tray – nothing to worry about? Well, that small leak can lead to massive dry rot problems throughout the property; and a simple drip under a drain could lead to foundation failure. I always warn people that the little problems turn into big problems.

On the flip side, you can be conned into paying for work that never needed doing in the first place. These cons tend to follow trends. For example, one that I came across frequently during one particular period , clients had been contacted by a company telling them they needed to have their concrete roof tiles painted. The problem, apparently, was that concrete tiles are porous...

I explain to my concerned clients that were the roof tile to be porous, it would soak up rainwater like a sponge whenever it rained, and then when the weather freezes, the tile would expand and crack. Instead these concrete tiles are made from a prescribed mix of concrete that is then compressed by a machine into the tile shape before being fired in a kiln at more than 900°. The tile is left to cool and then is fitted as a non-porous roof tile, able to withstand extreme temperatures at both ends of the scale.

However, you can easily see for yourself how successful this con has been - just drive round the streets and look at the houses and see how many roofs have been painted when they didn't need to be. The only thing that painting concrete roof tiles does is to change its appearance - it has absolutely no other effect whatsoever. And, as your little tour will show you, painting the tile when the next door's roof is not painted just makes your roof look odd. And I don't know what type of paint they are using but I do know that once it's been on for 12 months it begins to fade and peel off. Ask any paint specialist and they'll tell you that you cannot get a great bonding between paint and a concrete roof tile.

The truth about concrete roofs is that they last for a long time; the only problems that occur are the result of defective tiles or someone walking on the roof to fit an aerial or a satellite dish. However, this takes us neatly to four of the worst offenders for cons, incompetence and mis-sold products.

THE 4 BIG VILLAINS – DOUBLE GLAZING, FASCIAS, DAMP PROOFING and CENTRAL HEATING

#1 Double glazing: This home improvement leads to more problems than I care to mention, arising from the units themselves, the fitting and the naïve perception that a guarantee represents good quality work. If the job is carried out correctly, why should it need a guarantee – why should it go wrong?

Let's say you're fitting double glazing to a bay window; the big danger is that the bay will droop or even collapse. When wooden window frames were put into houses, particularly before 1985, they used to make up part of the structure. So along comes a window fitter who removes the window frame and finds that the brickwork drops. Down the line this leads to all sorts of defects including mortar cracks above and water ingress. And I find that in spite of being FENSA registered, which means the fitter has been approved to work to a particular standard and comply with building regulations, there are many companies that don't meet these requirements and leave their customers with future problems in the making.

FENSA registration isn't the only 'evidence' of competence that the customer relies on; people place far too much trust in guarantees too. A guarantee is not proof that the work has been done properly. Indeed, where it has, there is no need for a guarantee. For instance, I worked for a time at York Minster and can vouch for the fact that when the original glazing was put in place it managed to last around 1,000 years without any problems. Having said that, sealed double glazed units can and do fail, so a guaranteed of replacement is a useful thing to have.

Among the other window fitting defects I come across is not using lintels and then filling everything in with mastic; or sometimes the wall insulation slips out from one part of the structure but the fitters don't bother to re-install it.

To be fair, it is the labour that is at fault. Most of the modern window units themselves that are made today are of much better quality with tighter production controls in place. I'm also pleased to see that we are now moving towards triple glazed and even quadruple glazed window units; this is the way forward for modern housing standards.

Prices are variable too; and often the smaller but skilled builder can do a better job for much less cost. Some joinery stores and builders' merchants and even some DIY merchants can get plastic windows made up to a buyer's specifications and, from what I have seen, they are of very good quality. All there is on top of the unit cost is the labour for fitting, perhaps up to a day for a decent sized window. So, if you pay an average of £300 per window, how can some double glazing firms charge up to £9,000 for supplying and fitting a typical house with four windows at the front, four at the back and a couple down the side? The sums don't add up - clearly these companies are making an enormous profit.

#2 Fascias: Another common cold call from a building company will be to replace your fascia boards. The fascia board is the piece of wood that sits behind the guttering. If the gutter overhangs the wall it will usually have a wooden soffit unless it has open rafters. Some companies will come round and then clad that area with plastic and cut off the wooden timber that is rotten. That's all well and good because you don't have to paint it afterwards, but what they don't do is to install any ventilation; as a result the homeowner will then get condensation in their roof voids, causing a variety of defects including the corrosion of the roof timbers.

As I keep telling people, building is a science and it's about creating the right conditions and understanding the structure and forces involved as well as appreciating the 'ripple effect' that occurs should anything be changed on a particular property. Which takes us on neatly to villain #3 – treating damp.

#3 Damp treatment: For me one of the biggest jokes within the UK's building scene is how we treat damp. And with it comes a lot of opportunity to sell you remedies that you don't need or that simply don't work.

To explain this, we need to understand the humble brick. A house brick in the UK is about 255 mm long, 60 to 65 mm deep and 100 to 105 mm wide (it follows these dimensions so it can be handled easily). And a brick is also just a lump of clay that's been forced into a mould and then fired in a kiln. So if you pick up a brick and then cut it into slices you find you cannot blow through it from one side to the other because all of the cells within that slice are closed.

However, this does not stop some bright spark from coming along and saying that they can inject the brick with a chemical that will then damp proof it. I find this notion truly hilarious and because I am passionate about the building process, I've investigated this by cutting some of these treated bricks in half only to find that the injection doesn't do anything special at all. Instead it is the mortar that should be injected; the only process that works on the bricks themselves is to treat the surface of the internal wall to take away the dampness.

There is another ludicrous claim used to exploit concerned home-owners – resolving damp issues within a building by adding a wire to the property. This is called electro-osmosis; and whenever I have inspected a house with this system, it has been damp. That's because the process simply does not work.

The architectural solution to damp: Interestingly, there has been an effective protection against damp for centuries – the building overhang. Glebe barns – originally built alongside parish vicarages to store food grown in the glebe – typically have a piece of stone overhanging the wall, usually by about six inches. I have found only minimal damp problems with glebe barns. Nowadays we don't usually design buildings with an overhang running along the entire length of the building. However, a large overhang gives the building shading in the sun and also, more importantly, the walls do not get as wet and they do not lose as much heat as a result. The overhang also prevents the issue of rotting and keeps the windows clean.

By contrast, the modern design trend is to build property without any overhang whatsoever, so the walls and roof are flush with each other. And while in the past most windows were recessed into the wall because they looked better and because the builders knew they would be better protected, modern windows tend to be flush with the wall. This also, incidentally, increases external sound transmission.

You will only need a wind of 5 mph or less to bring the rain in at an angle towards a property, and you just need a hole the size of a full stop on this page for the wind to percolate that rainwater through and into the property. In the right weather, water will always find a way into a property from anywhere.

So, to my mind, we have not learned from history at all! In fact, we've allowed our own building practice to deteriorate even further in the pursuit of profit and nothing else.

#4 Central heating: It's easy to forget that central heating is a fairly recent invention. It's still common to buy a house built in the 1960s that does not have central heating. The trouble is that the installation of heating systems is fraught with problems and mistakes.

For example, I have come across many heating installations done by well-known companies where they have not put radiators underneath windows and not put in big enough radiators. This is basic stuff – and it means that the house may sometimes be warm enough but if there is a cold snap and the external temperature drops below 0°, the house will be cold, even when the heating is on full power.

This should not be such an issue in the 21st-century, not when they managed to do it so well millennia ago. The Romans managed to install brilliantly engineered under-floor heating; and they also had hot running water. And for other inspiring home-design features, you don't have to look further than the Minoans who lived in ancient Greece, particularly around Crete, and even the Incas. They put our modern efforts to shame and reveal them for what they are – ways to save money rather than giving people what they expect and deserve.

LOCATION AND SOCIAL TRENDS

The other building-related issue to bear in mind when buying a property is that it has probably had many other previous owners. In some areas the population is transient and houses are bought and sold on a regular basis so we are going to find a mishmash of botched jobs that bear little or no resemblance to professional building methods.

Anything from using textured coatings (some of which contain asbestos) to homeowners knocking out a chimney stack and then leaving the brickwork above it unsupported can spell big problems. You may also be concerned by the aesthetic impact of such previous 'improvements' and the expense you will face putting these right. The trend to knock out chimneys to enlarge a room can leave it without any comfortable focus; but correcting this can be troublesome. Knocking down wall that is load bearing is often a common problem. Unqualified builders (crooks) give home -owners the wrong advice in these situations, and avoid being found out by not apply for Building Regulations.

Let's appreciate too that older homes do not always mean they are trouble-free; far from it, although the problems with older properties tend to be design flaws rather than human error. You just have to go back to the 1930s to find houses with a lot of timbers built into the walls and they will have a lot of parapet walls. What frustrates me is that, with the passing of time, we do not get any better at making good quality properties and preventing defects from taking place. And I say this as a chartered builder.

Everyone involved in the building process, from the design stage through to the building and fitting out, shares responsibility, and it is an issue that should be a government responsibility. We need to learn from the builders of bye-gone days. The building pathology provides answers – it is all there to see. How come we have not learnt from previous building excellence?

Everyone knows they need a quality builder, but until we bring in licensed builders it will always be an unacceptable gamble. Builders need to be trained and they need to be approved and they need to be inspected, even if it's just once every five years. Critics of this may argue that we have building control officers already in place, but while they do a very good job they are not there to police builders, the building industry or the quality of work. Building control officers have a depth of knowledge that is second to none but unfortunately they are faced with builders who want to work quickly and get on with the next job.

Finally, just a quick note about the proliferation of websites that enable people to check on the qualities and qualifications of tradespeople and builders. I have not, so far, been impressed. I've been to several properties where a builder from a well-known recommending website has made a mess of the job they did.

I look forward to the day when licensing is brought in because the quality bona fide builder will pass any examination very easily while the cowboy builders and those without the experience will fail and will be drummed out of business.

STAY SAFE! And remember to use a local quality surveyor

If you're in the process of buying a house, what can you to do to stay safe given all these pitfalls? Well, it's not all bad news. If you understand just how unregulated our house building sector is, and just how easy it can be for a disreputable builder or building company to exploit your naivety, you're already one step ahead.

If you require advice on builders either use a qualified builder – apprentice served City & Guilds or a member of the Chartered Institute of Building – or ask a Chartered Surveyor or Chartered Building Engineer or other Chartered property professional. Personally I would question all other accolades used to persuade you of their worthiness.

When I visit a property I will automatically assume that everything is wrong until I am proved otherwise (you must do the same as a property buyer). You can imagine me visiting a property with two lights on my head: one is red and one is green. And until I have inspected it, every element within the property has a red light. Only when I have looked at it and approved it will that light turn to green.

I essentially inspect every potential defect one issue at a time, but I always look from another angle to see what else has been affected. The simple fact is that when you find a defect it usually means there's a chain involved with other defects relating to it in a separate part of the property.

If you're buying a new property, you must insist on obtaining a professional snag list. This will explain what defects a builder will or won't put right; and I would be very careful before buying a property with a snag list that protects the builder with too many get-out clauses. Let's remember that Edwardian and Victorian buildings are still standing today, so why shouldn't builders today have the confidence to build to the same quality?

A lot of these older properties have spectacular brickwork and roofs. But their builders did not have modern equipment such as hydraulic powered machines and they did not have power tools that can cut to the accuracy of 1,000th of an inch. Perhaps this is a part of the fundamental problem – not only are we not training our builders properly, but with so much automation there is simply not enough pride to be had in work done by hand.

LOOKING AHEAD

So, apart from introducing standard-regulating licensing, what is needed to improve the quality of houses we build? I have many ideas – here are just a couple (and there are more in section 4 of the book).

Building away from the site: I just don't understand why we don't build more prefabricated houses in factories and assemble them on site; this would massively increase quality control. The building of a house is the result of a huge amount of science, from how the structural loads can be dealt with to how the heat is distributed within the property. The more we can use laboratory precision the better will be the result.

Indeed, while I was writing this book, the insurance firm Legal and General (L&G), announced that it was investing in the largest flat pack homes factory in Europe which is found in North Yorkshire. Here, thousands of flat pack homes will be made and then transported around the UK and set down on plots of land. This is a popular way to create housing abroad and when it has been used in Britain, it's been a popular choice.

The idea is to provide those looking to get a foot onto the housing ladder with an effective means of doing so without resorting to traditional bricks and mortar. Another report published at the same time as L&G's, also noted that the UK has a shortage of workers with construction skills and we have no way of reaching the government's intention of building 200,000 new homes every year. However, with flat pack homes that target is potentially achievable.

It should also be noted that if the venture does prove successful then L&G will be investing in more factories to make pre-fabricated homes for assembly on site. I wholeheartedly believe the venture will be successful and it's long overdue to help make home creation in the UK not only easier to achieve but a reality too. Which brings me nicely onto my next big issue…

Dump the bricks: I want to finish this chapter by saying something radical that would help resolve many of the problems we find in our houses today; *we should stop building homes out of bricks.* Our houses of the future need to be radically redesigned with lots more insulation and appropriate modern materials; and they need to be as sustainable as possible which also means installing solar photovoltaic panels as well as solar hot water. But a good start would be to stop making them from bricks and mortar.

Part 3: Tips for navigating around the bigger problems when buying or selling

8: The surveyor's report explained

In my working life I visit lots of different properties every week and on arrival I'm often greeted by: "Have you come to do the valuation?"

My answer is always the same: "No, I have not - I have come to do the survey." And then the client will inevitably reply, "Well, it's the same difference, isn't it?"

No, it is not!

Essentially, a valuation is simply a certificate of lending that will confirm what the property is worth for lending purposes. So, while it might suit the bank's needs it means that a proper survey has not been undertaken - and the actual condition of the property being bought has not been evaluated. Logically it is impossible to determine a value until the condition has been fully assessed through a proper survey.

By contrast, a survey report does reveal the condition of the property. However, there are several different types of survey available, and to become a smart buyer you need to pick the one that's right for the property you're considering. The biggest mistake you can make is to try to save a small sum of money by opting for an inferior inspection; it could cost you tens of thousands of pounds down the line!

So let's examine each option, starting with the basic level – the valuation

VALUATION

The Council of Mortgage Lenders' Guidelines clearly state, "The valuation should be carried out by a Chartered Surveyor who is a member of the RICS". However, a valuation is effectively an opinion on what a property is worth for mortgage purposes; and like opinions, valuations are subjective. Two surveyors inspecting the same property may, inevitably, come up with two slightly different valuations, particularly if they are from out of the area, a practice that is frowned upon. I have even seen valuations that have been £30-£40,000 apart for the same property.

Also, most of these valuation reports are done under nondisclosure criteria, which means that the person paying for the report will not be told the official valuation of the property. This can hide price distortion where some properties are valued too high because, for example, the vendor is insisting on a higher asking price.

Many bank surveyors don't even sign their name on the report; instead they insert an electronic signature that does not properly identify them or their qualifications. If you received a letter signed with a number would you trust it?

So, why would anyone settle for a valuation instead of a survey? Sadly, the truth is that they are badly advised, often by banks.

For instance, I recently went to a house where I could literally insert my iPhone in the cracks between some of the bricks. These cracks were running from top to bottom on the external brickwork in one wall. I looked around and wasn't surprised to see the root of the problem, a very large tree close to the property.

The elderly lady selling the house was asking when she could move, and I had to break it to her that it was unlikely she would be moving at all. Pointing out the massive cracks I asked whether she had buildings' insurance. She replied that she had not, and explained that she had only bought the house five years earlier. So I asked about the survey that she'd had: "I didn't get a survey done," she replied, "because I was told I didn't need one."

I was astonished. Essentially, someone within that property buying process who should have known better gave her terrible, unprofessional advice. As a direct result, she is now stuck with a property she cannot sell and is looking at living her days out there or having to rent it out. It is an extreme scenario but not unusual – and definitely not acceptable.

There are lots of reasons for getting a valuation report done, such as for matrimonial, probate, inheritance tax, or pension reasons; but when buying any property, you need a lot more information than a valuation will provide. Why risk tens of thousands of your hard-earned pounds for the small sum saved by opting for a basic valuation?

GENERAL SURVEY

The next level is a middle offering and consists of a general survey. Many people are drawn to this as it clearly includes some detailed examination but isn't too expensive. However, there can be problems with this level of inspection, and increasingly they are the result of some companies (particularly on-line organisations) trying to increase profit margins by minimising the detail. And you need to be extremely careful about using on-line survey comparison prices websites – they often take a large percentage of your fee.

Some surveyors use templates based on the traffic light system; it makes it easier to complete the report but can leave it open to too much interpretation. Many people, having sought this type of inferior report, come to me for help to understand it, but of course without having inspected the property myself, it is almost impossible. I do not like this system and prefer to use a completely different format which involves common sense and saying what we want to say i.e. reporting the facts. The final report should reflect everything clearly that was included in the level of survey.

This is why the reports from my own surveying business can be at least 6,000 words long while other surveyor's basic reports sometime barely reach 1,000 words. And even the most articulate surveyor will often struggle to present a fair report in such few words.

STRUCTURAL SURVEY

The next level up is for a full structural survey, until recently called a building survey. This is the most in-depth report a buyer can get – or so you might think. There are property professionals offering what they call a structural survey; whilst our own structural surveys run to a good 40 pages, theirs are only a few pages – often as few as three. And they don't include all the additional annotations and photographs that we add; nor does the surveyor necessarily meet the buyer on site.

Now, I'm not saying that you should always automatically go for the top level survey; I think it's just as important to make sure you get what you think you're getting – as only then can you make meaningful use of the report, whatever level you've paid for.

There's another reason to invest in a good survey. When you come to sell the property, you can use it to show a clear history of how you have improved and repaired the property since buying it. Think of it like selling a car with a full service history.

HOW TO GET MORE FROM YOUR SURVEY

When you know what can potentially be hidden by an inadequate inspection, it is easier to ask for more information. So if, for example, you commission a structural survey and receive a five-page report, you know there must be detail that is missing; the property professional has probably only reported on what they can easily see, not on whether the property is in fact about to fall down. (At the time of writing, we are helping a customer who paid a surveyor £2,000 for what he thought was a detailed report but now finds his house has massive problems with the foundations, something missed in the report he commissioned).

This is why we are often commissioned to deliver a 'defect report' to supplement inadequate property inspection reports. A client might have paid for a valuation and been advised in the report of cracks, with the recommendation to consult an expert such as a chartered engineer or a chartered building engineer. We will then go along and write that report for the client. Similarly, we can be asked to comment on a surveyor's report that notes there is damp in the property. The report doesn't go into any detail so our task is to diagnose the extent of the problem.

Of course this is the standard of work you should expect *as a matter of course* from your survey, if only all surveys were done in more detail.

Worse still are the big companies that offer structural surveys, only to inform you in the expensive report you have just paid for that you now need to appoint a structural surveyor to examine some specific issues. Surely, you think, 'that is what I've just paid for?'

Whenever I have questioned a report like this I have always been told that the property inspector concerned is not available to comment; behind this lies the fact that although they sell you a structural survey, it is not carried out by someone sufficiently qualified. Indeed, in many cases the surveyor is not qualified at all.

So, to sum up, members of the public are simply being hoodwinked by poor practices. It is wrong – and now you know so, as well as deciding after all to pay for a more detailed survey, you can ask some very pertinent questions before appointing your surveyor. Remember to look for the professional accreditations, and don't forget the importance of using a local surveyor who knows the area well.

And always appoint the local surveyor directly; don't go through a third party. Your surveyor should be there to serve *you*, not someone else.

9. Choosing the right location and house

We all live much more mobile lives than we used to – and this is reflected in our house buying. In the old days, people tended to stay in the same area for most of their lives. Nowadays, with new jobs, school catchment areas and, of course, the investment potential of our new house to consider, we're venturing further afield. And choosing the right *location* is just as important as choosing the right house.

So, what should you look for? What factors tell you that the location is a safe bet?

Money and convenience

Value for Money

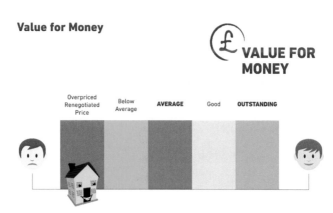

The one thing you don't want to do is lose money on your house, so the trick is to choose an up-and-coming area where your investment will grow in value faster than elsewhere. But you also need essential conveniences – the facilities and amenities that will sustain your day-to-day life.

For instance, if you have a young family then you will need to be near schools, public transport, shops and maybe good community medical services. You're probably going to want plenty of other young families around too, and not be isolated.

What about commuting? Maybe you're looking for a location that will reduce your daily commute to a round-trip of 30 miles along country roads – but are you sure those roads don't get congested by 100 other commuters doing the same, or the daily convoy of delivery vehicles from a nearby depot?

And what about farmers – you've fallen in love with a delightful little farming hamlet and everyone says that farmers are really friendly. We can't live without our farmer's as they are essential to our economy – but will you mind the mess, noise and delays caused because the main street is the only way to get from one field to another? Some positively enjoy this, but others may not.

Even something as simple as a lamp post can be a make-or-break factor; let's say you've found the perfect street with good neighbours, a small shop etc. – but you didn't notice the street lamp directly in front of the house that attracts local teenagers most evenings to hold impromptu street parties...

You see, there are always things that the house-seller's brochure won't reveal. I have seen over and over again how often people do not take enough time and trouble to find out more about the area they're planning to move to. And of course, the other crucial question, and one that can prove very expensive and can wreck people's lives, is *will you be able to sell the property when you're ready to move on?* One visit and a couple of questions in the local pub will not be enough.

So, what does the Smart Buyer do?

A smart buyer will be deliberately looking for these issues, and that means asking an independent surveyor to help. With nothing to lose, an independent surveyor will tell the buyer the good, the bad and the ugly truths about the property *and* where it is located. Unlike a bank surveyor, you will be able to cross-examine your own surveyor *and* trust in what you're told. And you'll be helped to look into other potential nightmares...

Geology and infrastructure

Fracking is the new horror-on-the-block, and one I'm particularly concerned about. Whatever your views on energy policy, fracking is tantamount to creating an earthquake and having experienced one myself in Nepal and seen how fragile the ground can be, it baffles me that fracking and its potential problems are so glossed over. For house-buyers, proximity to a proposed fracking site is serious.

New rail routes are another important consideration. There's no doubt that the upcoming HS2 development to create a high-speed railway link between London, the Midlands and the North is going to cause a lot of disturbance to a lot of people. However, a property within ten minutes of a new HS2 railway station could also be a great investment and might rocket in value. And even with an existing line, the trains whizz past in only a few seconds and you may not be bothered at all by them; remember, however, that your future potential purchasers may not be so agreeable.

Soldiers, churches and airplanes...

No, not the title of a new Hollywood comedy but three more potential problems your independent surveyor will be on the look out for:

Military bases can be good news as they attract good community facilities. But maybe being woken by early-morning shooting practice, tank manoeuvres or marching band practice isn't your thing? Best to ask some questions.

Churches are mixed blessings to the home-buyer and I always advise caution. There are the obvious issues such as weddings, funerals, christenings etc. – and all the attendant parking, bustle and bell ringing. But there's also a potentially very serious problem if your house sits within the church boundaries – the ancient rules about Chancel and roof repairs mean you may find that you are obliged to make a contribution to the repair costs! You can get additional insurance to cover this but there are instances where people have been unable to sell their houses because of this ancient rule. Ask your solicitor to perform a Chancel check.

Aeroplanes are not just a problem for the South-East; you may only have a small, local airfield some 40 miles away – but how noisy are the planes, what is their usual direction to and from the airfield, and what times of the day do they fly?

The Smart Buyer's location checklist

1. Visit the property at different times of day (though an internal inspection is not necessary every time)

2. Visit three or four separate times on a weekend

3. Meet the local surveyor on-site at the time of inspection

4. Meet & greet your would-be neighbours – you could find out all kinds of things that will influence your view of the property and location

5. Remember - a drive-by alone is not enough, but it *can* reveal lots of information about the property and the area.

So, location is as big an issue as the house itself, maybe even more important. And a Smart Buyer will always do as much research as possible and seek reliable independent advice. You'll also see why it's best to take all those TV programmes about buying the 'perfect house' with a very large pinch of salt; they make you fall in love with the property itself and the view from the kitchen window, but how often do you hear them discussing minerals, war-games and church roofs? Makes you think doesn't it...

10. Buying/selling from probate, auction and divorce.

Many houses are sold as a result of particular life circumstances, and sometimes they are sold by auction for a swift closure. Buyers shouldn't overlook these sources of potentially great houses, although if you spot what looks like a bargain, there's usually a reason for it. And I've seen many a house at auction go for *more* than its true market value. A smart buyer will always try to find out as much as possible about *why* a house is being sold. And sellers should also be aware of the pitfalls of being too greedy.

HOUSES BEING SOLD UNDER PROBATE

Where there's a will, there's often a family! And that's why these houses can be troublesome purchases simply because there is often a whole group of people with an interest in the sale and reaching agreement on any price negotiation is tricky. So buyers need to be aware that buying from probate can be a frustratingly long process. Sellers, however, should take note too; you can lose a lot of money by digging your heels in. In my experience, the sad truth is that many families fall out during probate sales, whether about the responsibilities, the asking price or the buyer, and this can make the process difficult and drawn out.

As an example, a recent property I visited was for a house being sold under probate for £185,000 and the buyer wanted to reduce the asking price to £175,000. That's a drop of £10,000 and, by chance, there were 10 members of the family waiting to carve up the sale proceeds. So it would have amounted to only losing £1,000 each, but the family would not accept the offer. The buyer then ended negotiations and that property was still on the market several months later. What made this even more ridiculous was that the property was in fact in very poor condition; under any other circumstances an individual seller would probably have been delighted with such an offer.

Another probate property I remember was valued at £1.1 million. A buyer came along who was genuinely interested in purchasing the property and negotiated the asking price down to £900,000. Again, there were five or six family members involved in the process and they refused to accept the new offer. That particular buyer also walked away from negotiations as did a second buyer; when the house was eventually sold, by auction, it went for only £750,000.

So, with probate if you're buying be patient and don't be surprised by unreasonable rejections of your offer; and if you're selling, don't hang around waiting for the perfect offer – it may never come. If you are involved in selling a probate property please consider my very sensible advice above.

Once you have made the plunge and decided to buy a house at Auction or from an estate under probate or maybe a house as a result of divorce, talk to your local surveyor first.

Good surveyors will spend time talking to you and providing advice because after all you will require a survey.

Prior to calling us make your notes in the space below.

HOUSES BEING SOLD AT AUCTION

Many surveyors view a house being sold at auction as effectively a 'forced sale'; i.e. someone usually wants to sell the property quickly. And certainly, at an auction once the hammer goes down that's it; no renegotiations – it's a sale.

As a surveyor of many years standing, the best piece of advice I can give is to be very careful of buying by auction. It's fast; sometimes there's bidding 'off the wall' where someone is bidding by telephone so you can't see what's going on; and often there are some pretty nasty reasons why the sale is being hurried. I have never seen a straightforward house being sold at auction. Never. Whenever I have surveyed houses being sold by auction, I have always found a string of issues to be dealt with. Some may be major, others minor, but there are usually a lot of them.

So, while the dreamer will see a 'gorgeous' house for auction and anticipate a cheap price and just go for it, a smart buyer will typically ask me to survey the property before the auction. Remember, you can sell any old thing at auction quite legally by "selling as seen".

"It looks just like a chocolate box cottage!"

I remember a very pretty little house up for auction. It really did look stunning from the outside. However, from the moment I stepped from my car, I adopted my surveyor mindset and began a visual inspection of the property, looking at everything from gutters, drains and cracks to whether the house was actually the right shape.

I began to smell a rat and thought to myself: "This is not right." To this day, I'm still not entirely sure what it was that alerted me but I knew something was wrong. Inside the house I pulled the carpets back and found all the floors were rotten; someone had just put a thin layer of plywood over the entire floor. Further inspection revealed a number of other dodgy tricks, including propping the floor up. The whole house was, frankly, a mess.

Of course, buyers will always be drawn to auctions – often the houses are empty, they're not in a chain and the expectation is that they will go for a song. But the question you must always ask is: *"Why is this house being sold – and at this price guide?"*

What appears to be a bargain price might actually be the going rate in that precise area; or perhaps the house itself is fine but there are some 'hidden' issues about the local area (see chapter 9).

HOUSES BEING SOLD FOR DIVORCE

Sometimes you spot a great-looking house on the market and the estate agent tells you a sad story about the owners divorcing and needing to sell it. Your instinct might tell you that they are bound to be looking for a quick sale – however, this is another situation where you need to go in with your eyes open and anticipate problems.

As with probate, you are usually dealing with more than one seller; in addition, it is possible, even likely, that those sellers are not on the best of terms and will not easily be able to agree price negotiations with the agent. And each party in the divorce may have separate lawyers involved who are trying to maximise the price as part of the divorce settlement.

Even in an amicable divorce, the process can take longer simply because two selling parties are involved, but often in these cases they are just as keen as you are for a swift conclusion.

Be aware however that houses sold because of divorce usually end up going for their market value.

11. Understanding builder's estimates.

What happens after receiving your detailed expert survey report? You sit down to decide on which repairs need doing when, and what the cost will be. So, understanding builders' estimates – or at least how they try to put them together – is a vital part of deciding on your final offer for that property. The trouble is that, in our unregulated building profession, estimates can be very misleading.

Home Improvement

Improve your home

Modernised Doors ☐

New Tiling ☐

Wall Cavity Repairs ☐

Fixtures & Fittings ☐

Carpets & Flooring ☐

Decorating ☐

Painting ☐

Home Improvement

In recent years I had a stand at the 'Self Build Show'. People would approach me to discuss their ideas for a barn conversion or an extension; and the single most common question they would ask was: "What is the price for this per square metre? " Seems reasonable doesn't it? After all you're probably sitting there with architects' plans, so it is the obvious guideline to ask for.

Estimating a cost based on area measurements should be a mathematical process. Measure a ceiling; you know how much plasterboard you need, how much plaster, and if necessary the length of joists above. So it should be no problem to work out an accurate cost that will not vary significantly for materials from quote to quote.

Indeed, the proper way to estimate how much a particular job will cost is to calculate the quantities. For instance, you probably don't know, but the number of standard bricks in a square metre of wall is 59.9. And a skilled bricklayer will take between 45 and 75 minutes to lay a square metre of bricks, depending on the conditions. So, the cost should be a simple calculation, yes?

Well, I have to shatter that fantasy and tell you that many builders' estimates are frankly worthless. I have seen lots of builder's estimates in my time as a Chartered Surveyor and Chartered Builder and many are just unbelievable. Some builders have been known to calculate the cost of work and double it. For example, a client of mine was planning an extension on his house consisting of a kitchen, a toilet and a utility room downstairs, and a bedroom and a bathroom upstairs. He showed me the range of five different builders' estimates he had been offered, and they varied between £65,000 to £130,000. How can it be possible to explain an increase of 100% from the lowest to the highest – for identical work?

I questioned each of the builders about how they had calculated their estimates. Because they had not, at that stage, been told who had been selected for the job they were happy to talk to me.

Some simply told me that they remembered back to a previous job, checked into the square metre price they had charged and based the estimate on that. The builder who was awarded the project, however, had calculated his quote in the good old-fashioned way, working out the hours he would take, adding a small percentage on top of materials and ensuring a basic profit percentage. This for me is the way all builders should calculate a price for a particular job.

Unfortunately, many builders are not professional tradespeople; and their abilities when it comes to estimating costs are as questionable as their work standards. After all, if a builder has never served an apprenticeship with a truly skilled master, how will they have learned how to calculate a quote? Remember, the builder's estimate needs to be very detailed, and those estimates that include material quantities have a better prospect of being correct.

CHOOSING A BUILDER YOU CAN TRUST

Builder Projects

Can the property be extended?

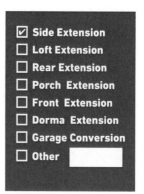

There's simply too much at stake to appoint a builder after only a chance meeting – but some people do! Do not forget that you are allowing the builder into your life as well as your home. And we've all heard horror stories about job costs suddenly spiralling upwards.

Spiralling costs should never happen in my opinion for two very good reasons – the job should be overseen by a suitably qualified professional whose quote will be an accurate one, and with this there will be no nasty surprises so most building contracts can then be on a fixed-price basis.

A simple solution is to hire a chartered surveyor to organise any work that needs to be done. Not only will the surveyor write the specification (including costs), they will also supervise the work undertaken and ensure it's done to the proper standards.

So how do you find your builder? I am very suspicious of the websites that have sprung up trying to give people peace of mind based on past customers' testimonials (or an arbitrary star-based appraisal system). Instead, I recommend whenever possible to find recommendations from family and friends, people you can trust and whose work you can see for yourself.

You should also examine the way the estimate is presented. I know you're paying for building expertise, but if an estimate for a £65,000 job is presented on a scrappy piece of paper, badly spelled and with very little detail, be suspicious. You have every right to demand a detailed breakdown of work, time and costs. I recommend that you employ a professional i.e. a Chartered Building Engineer, Chartered Building Surveyor or Architect as an adviser when you're selecting a builder.

BEWARE OF THE LARGE CORPORATE BUILDERS

There may be some very good companies around, but there are many larger corporate firms that offer a scandalous level of customer service and poor building quality. These are the firms that, for example, offer to fix a home's damp, fix the drains, fit a boiler or fix the windows. In many cases these are franchised operations, and I would warn everyone to be extremely careful before engaging their services. They are also the hard sellers, preying on naïve or vulnerable people. Many simply want to replace an item when in fact it could be repaired.

For example, a customer phoned me concerned about an estimate from one of these companies of £3,500 for supplying and fitting a new gas boiler. Within a few minutes, I had found a local plumber just two streets away from where she lived, who turned up to replace her boiler for £1,200. The plumber showed me his invoice; the boiler had cost £720 plus VAT, and he completed the entire job within one day. That company was going to make huge profit by exploiting my client. So it pays to be vigilant, shop around and go local.

The other danger with franchise operations is when you contact them directly yourself, for example to solve some damp problems, without even looking at your property they will convince you that: "Of course you have a problem, sir; and we know exactly what it is and we can sell you a damp proof course." They must have a crystal ball.

Another scandalous trick in the 1980s and 1990s was to sell unnecessary cavity wall tie repairs. A butterfly cavity wall tie or metal strip was used to bridge the inner and outer walls. These items were not galvanised or made from stainless steel, and when they rusted they expanded, causing minor cracks in the brickwork. This was then the cue for a disreputable company to declare the building as losing some of its 'integrity' and in need of new ties. However, my firm gets to see these houses when we are asked to check for cavity wall tie failure. And what we find is shocking.

We drill a hole in the wall and then use an endoscopic camera, a bigger version of the sort used in a hospital. This reveals exactly what is going on inside the wall. While a very few properties did need new ties, most that I looked at had not failed at all; there were just totally unnecessary additional ties installed.

The other issue I have is with larger firms offering damp proof courses. Some of this work is indeed necessary – but some of it is not. This is why it is so important to use local firms; as well as being more reliable and honest, they have a local reputation to protect. Most of these local operators will be straightforward to deal with and tell a homeowner exactly what needs to be done. By contrast, larger and franchised firms will detail all kinds of extras that 'need doing' such as lifting floorboards and knocking down walls, all or most of which is unnecessary except to support their guarantee. But as many of us know, getting some firms to honour these guarantees can be almost impossible, rendering them worthless. And as I've said before, if the work is done right in the first place who needs a guarantee?

12. Working with Estate Agents.

Estate Agents are in my view unfairly often maligned by all of us: "If I could buy/sell without using one, I would!" Well, in my professional opinion a good estate agent is worth every penny. The trouble is that there are plenty around that are not very good and this adds to the profession's poor image. So, this short chapter will help sellers to assess an agent and find the right one; and if you're buying you will know if and when to push the agent harder on your behalf.

Never use on-line estate agents!

Yes, they may look impressive – and they may undercut your local estate agent. But they tend to under price your property too. And when we're surveying, they can be hard to get hold of for access to the property. It is always much better when the agent meets us at the property with a key, or uses a key safe, as quite a few good ones do here in York and Leeds.

Remember, if something seems cheap, there is always a reason!

THE ADVANTAGES OF GOING LOCAL

At the time of writing, the number of firms advertising on television to sell properties is growing. This worries me; they are effectively online agents and their popularity comes from their ability to undercut the fees charged by High Street agents. Now, plenty of local estate agents will make extensive use of the internet – that's not the problem. It's the lack of local knowledge that means the online companies often deliver truly inferior service.

It's not uncommon to come across London based companies advertising on TV in Yorkshire to sell your house for you. Now their fee might look tempting but first consider this: they are not local, they do not live locally, they do not have a direct investment in the local economy, and they may know little about house prices in specific local areas. They can also try to sell you other services such as conveyancing; so then you have both an agent and a solicitor, neither of whom have that valuable local knowledge.

I have to confess that I am appalled by the practices I have encountered with some of these national online estate agents. I have seen many houses being <u>sold at well below the market value for the area.</u> They probably do this because they want to get a fast fee. And indeed, a number of online estate agents are suspiciously keen that there is no survey carried out on the property. Why? It's because a survey might reveal issues that need to be negotiated, creating delays to that sought-after quick fee.

Sometimes however it may just be ignorance; after all, if you're sat in your London office with no professional knowledge of the Leeds housing market, how can you possibly assess the value of a property there? Websites would give you a rough estimate, but that's it – no local insight to get you to a true and accurate figure. And the market fluctuates - this requires an estate agent to be strategic in pricing either at the lower end of a rising market or at the top end of that market.

LAZY *vs* PROFESSIONAL

Local does not, of course, automatically mean better. So when looking locally, you need to know what standards you can expect too. After all, agents are salespeople; their job is to sell, and that involves hard work. Most agents I know are really well qualified and experienced.

As an example, in one particular Yorkshire town there is an estate agent that sells more properties than any other because they are professional. Whenever I go into their offices they have all of the property details on display with full details on hand (you'd be surprised by how lazy some agents are at supplying basic information). The staff there are well trained – they are not pompous or patronising; they are well-informed about their properties; they can answer any question you might ask. Quite often these are also family-run businesses - and they sell more houses because of their thorough, friendly yet professional approach.

Contrast this with a recent visit (sadly typical) to a branch of a national franchise. It happened also to be my own third repeat visit, each time hoping to pick up the keys to the same property only to be told they weren't in the office. A potential buyer walked in, quite obviously looking seriously for a house. He asked for some simple information and the reply he got was: "I don't know."

And that was it. Instead of "Give me a minute and I will find out for you," it was just an unprofessional closure of the conversation. I find it hard to believe that the staff in an agency cannot memorise the stock they have and the basic details, let alone show some enthusiasm for helping a customer; surely this should be the basic requirement of the job? Go local and save time, money and hassle.

However, if you are a smart buyer and you come across an estate agent who cannot be bothered to give you the basic information, don't walk away; you can use this to your advantage. For instance, if the agent is unfamiliar with the property and your survey has revealed some serious problems you are in a position of strength to suggest that the price is wrong and needs to be reconsidered.

I'm a
SMART
House Buyer

The benefit of mystery shopping...

I once built a new house and put it on the market with an estate agent. However, shortly afterwards, we 'mystery shopped' them and were appalled by the level of customer service. Just as bad as the incorrect information they gave us about my house: "It's only three bedrooms and there's no garage." Well, having built the house, I knew this was wrong!

After switching estate agents, I sold the property shortly afterwards. And another time I sold a house, the agency sent not one but *three* of their agents to view the property and be fully prepared for selling it. This ensured that whoever spoke to a potential buyer could talk about the house on a personal level. This local family-run business gets my vote.

So the moral of the story is that 'local' ticks one box, but 'professionalism' is the other box that absolutely must be ticked. The fee you pay is for their excellent service, so make sure you get it.

THE CHALLENGE OF ACCURATE HOUSE PRICING

The Price Target for House Buying

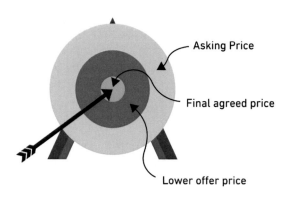

I mentioned earlier that remote national companies can lack sufficient local knowledge to price a property correctly. However, even with a local agent, some buyers are not happy; I often get clients who complain about the price their agent has recommended. There is a careful balance to be struck when it comes to deciding the price of a property; should it be vendor-led or should it be a true reflection of its market worth?

The answer should be a simple one: ultimately the right price is a market price, not a theoretical one – it's what someone is prepared to pay for the property. So the open market value of a property in reasonable condition is defined by a willing buyer and a willing seller concluding an arm's length transaction after a proper period of marketing. That's when a seller can expect to command the optimum price.

There is a new trend that confuses pricing further and can create artificial price tags – "banding". A lot of estate agents are banding their house prices, when publicising them on property portals. But houses are individual items, and have individual value to the people who possess or aspire to possessing them. And an asking price is an invitation to make an offer – it's a starting point.

However, some kind of benchmarking is useful; measuring up a house, calculating the floor area and then comparing with similar properties in the same area can be a good guide to a true price for that postcode.

Of course there is a flaw with this. Some of the new two-bedroom houses that are being built are around 5% smaller than similar houses were 10 or 15 years ago. Developers are reducing the floor area of the properties they are building, and this means that important features such as the number and size of cupboards and other storage areas is also reduced.

The Price Negotiation

So, estate agents are vital – and you have every right to expect the best professional service from them. I've put together a checklist to help you select the right one when selling, and get them working harder when buying.

ESTATE AGENTS – WHY NOT SEE IF YOU QUALIFY FOR THE "SMART AGENTS BADGE" by contacting the author!

Jon's top tips for choosing estate agents:

- Use your local estate agent whenever possible

- Visit the local estate agent and ask them how many houses they have sold recently

- Do not be critical about estate agent fees but ask what service is included – you want value for money

- When selling, ensure the agent has a good location for their branch and good local knowledge

- Inspect their marketing literature

- Check out their website and how easy it is to use and navigate.

- Meet as many of their staff as you can – check they are approachable and easy to talk to.

As a final word, have you ever bought a new car? Or even a quality used one? If so, you'll know that you are well looked after in the showroom, with cups of tea and lots of attention. So why are there still some estate agents who look down at their desk and try to appear invisible when you come through the door? Don't they want to sell houses?

Come on estate agents, offer cups of tea and coffee to your customers - and surveyors too!

Part 4: Campaigning for a healthier housing market.

I am both an active campaigner for change and a vociferous commentator on the housing market. For example, we have the Land Registry but data from this can sometimes be misleading as it doesn't refer to floor area, which to some buyers is as important as number of owners and mileage is to a car buyer. So I have been campaigning for years to create a national house price database. This would be for houses properly examined by chartered surveyors that can then provide an accurate average price for every type of house in every postcode in the UK.

In this final section, I share some of my thoughts and efforts to change the bigger problems and address the enormous challenges that we face in this country in terms of buying houses and recording prices.

Now, I'm a Yorkshireman, and I don't waste time or breath on vanity projects. So all of this is straightforward doable stuff. It just takes people with guts and common sense. Unfortunately, within our politics they seem to be few and far between. But maybe someone with influence will read this, see just how daft it is that we continue as we do, and make something happen. Maybe...

Domestic Product Growth

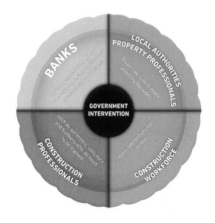

13: Lenders need to change

Our first-time-buyer market is increasingly relying on the 'Bank of Mum and Dad'. Not only does this exclude those who don't have this option; it also shows that banks are missing out on commercial opportunities. I talk in this section about 'banks' but much of this applies to all forms of mortgage lender.

I have already mentioned the drawbacks of bank valuations (see chapter 5); however, behind this lies a more serious trend and one that should be exposed in what is supposed to be an era of clean, transparent banking, the antithesis of immoral or dangerous gambling.

Some banks use what they call an 'automated valuation model' (AVM); they consider a property remotely without sending in an inspector and simply apply algorithms to decide on its value. Other banks just use 'drive-by' valuations where no one even gets out of the car to look at the house. The cruel irony is that during the recession, banks were repossessing properties they had no doubt previously valued by this method! Offering a mortgage on these types of valuation is no better than gambling – but it's *your* future, prosperity and quality of life that is being gambled.

Now, why is this allowed? Well, believe it or not it is enabled by legislation. You see, there are laws in place – the Banks' and Building Societies' Act amongst others – that require a lender to acquire a certificate of valuation before being allowed to lend against a property. But in addition to its original purpose, making sure that uncertified loans are not made, it is being used to allow lenders to fast track mortgages on the basis of wholly inadequate property information. The Banking Act needs to be altered so that a more detailed inspection is needed. And of course we have one already; it's called a survey. Remember, condition equates to value - if it has defects it's worth a lot less.

This has to change. We need to ask - and be answered – why banks are allowed to maintain their current lending practices; why they haven't learned from their disastrous business models of the recent global recession; and why they are leaving themselves wide open once again to being sued for the shady way they add the cost of the valuation and other fees to the mortgage to maximise their interest earnings? And why are they still not required to inform and clarify to every customer that he or she is free to appoint their own surveyor?

It is always easy to be nostalgic for a better time years ago, but believe me, there were once better times. I often speak to retired chartered surveyors who remember the good old days when they had excellent relationships with local bank managers. Everything was conducted locally; everyone knew everyone; and everyone worked together for the good of the customers (both sellers and buyers), not just for greed and profit.

By contrast, look at today's sharp practice with banks passively making it difficult to appoint your own preferred solicitor or surveyor. If you do what they want by accepting the one *they* recommend, they often fail to point out that there may be a fee for you being referred. Peter Gibson shares his own solicitor's perspective on this in the final section of the book – and I recommend you read what he has to say!

It also saddens me that during the recession the banks chose to evict people who had fallen into mortgage arrears rather than seeking an alternative that allowed the owners to remain such as lease-back. Banks used to be essential and valued facilitators for building businesses and building lives; now it seems they are simply in it for profit at any human cost.

So it's no surprise then that people don't trust banks. However, people are also still in awe of banks, despite the new 'friendly faces' that greet you in High Street branches. Faced with a complex bank procedure, people tend to do what they are told (and never challenge it) and if that means helping generate even more profit for the bank, what incentive is there for the bank to change?

14: Changing how we sell houses

The process of selling a home in the UK is fundamentally flawed. The problems begin when the home seller invites five different estate agents to assess the property and get five different selling recommendations. The prices usually vary widely and many buyers are drawn to the agent suggesting the highest; often however this will be the national chain agent with poor local knowledge of prices and trends. The result is a market that gets stuck, chains that break and lots of unnecessary (and often expensive) heartache. Things could be a lot better if we made some changes to how we sell houses.

Did you know...

1 There are many UK national estate agents that are part of a large group of companies that have their own surveying business? However, it is not made transparent to the seller, buyer, mortgagee or home owner that the bank, the estate agent and the surveyor are all part of the same company – and I think this is conflict of consumer interest. This explains why...

2 Some pundits have suggested that surveyors have been under duress to value up property in order to increase the size of the mortgage. If true, the unsustainable price increase certainly contributed to the price crash and to the world recession. And...

3 Remember that it was you and I – hard working members of the public – who suffered, not the bankers.

As we saw in the section on buying houses from probate and divorces (chapter 10), overly optimistic price targets just lead to delayed selling and ultimately a disappointment. And this is why the single most effective improvement to the way we sell houses would be the seller's survey.

Yvette Cooper MP, as housing minister in the Labour Government, wanted to introduce a Vendor Report, bringing the selling process for England and Wales closer to that of Scotland. However, this will only work if supervised by suitably qualified chartered surveyors, otherwise you will still have poor assessments that lead to price arguments and ill-advised purchases.

Unfortunately, the government of the day came up instead with the grand idea that you could be trained in only three months to conduct Vendor Reports. To put this into perspective, I spent 10 years developing my knowledge of property enough to be able to offer an expert opinion on defects and problems. The government's three-month training was barely even an NVQ level II process!

But, as with so many sensible government ideas, they pulled the plug shortly before it went live or could be further developed. The idea remains a good one and it is an excellent opportunity to allow chartered surveyors, architects and building engineers to bring their expertise more fully to the heart of the housing market. Try telling that to any government though!

If we followed Scotland's lead and insisted on a survey before an offer is made, the whole process would move much more smoothly and much faster. My own philosophy is to work as much as I can for both parties – buyer and seller – in using my expertise to evaluate a sale accurately and achieve a satisfactory outcome for all concerned.

In the meantime, if you are about to sell your house, there are ways to tap your property professional for useful advice. When you show them round the house, ask what you can do to help sell the house. It may mean redecorating or even fitting a new basic kitchen, or simply getting round at last to repairing that hole in the plaster above the kitchen door.

And being able to report, with documentation such as an old survey report, on any recent work done makes valuers really happy! But of course, best of all is to get an independent survey and base your entire selling process on this, starting with a realistic valuation of your property in its current state and in the current market.

15: Stop building the wrong houses

In a nutshell, we are not only building insufficient numbers of new houses; we're not building enough first-time buyer houses and at the right price. But I believe the problem goes much deeper than this; simply addressing numbers will get more houses into circulation – but will they be fit for purpose as we move swiftly towards the mid-twenty-first century?

Modular building: I mentioned earlier that the whole way we build houses is out of date. We have the skills and technology now to create most of a house off-site, building in a modular way. With this comes the opportunity to research, develop and standardise modern improvements in our housing to make them better fit for purpose in this era of climate change and unpredictable energy costs. But there are other benefits to this way of building, ones that impact directly on the experience of the owner.

In the US they already have the ability to pick up their house, put it on the back of a trailer and move it to a new location. This means that the initial investment can stay within a family even when living circumstances change. Why can't we simply sell plots of land and allow people to install their own house (with the help of a local team of architect, surveyor and approved builder)?

Energy: We continue to build styles of houses that evolved in different times, pre-central heating. Times and priorities have changed and these are simply no longer suitable.

Energy costs are rising all the time but we continue to build houses that are not as energy efficient as they could be. Our approach to the problem is like closing the stable door after the horse has bolted. We patch up and retro-fit new innovations but these are compromises at best.

Living in the northern hemisphere, in a maritime climate, we really need to think more about energy conservation. In a perfect housing world, all new homes would be built to a high sustainable standard. They wouldn't be so reliant on fossil fuels; they would be able to generate their own energy from solar, thermal, wind and air source pumps. And they would have ultra-modern efficient insulation.

Smart buyers today have worked out that a house that is not energy-efficient will be worth less in years to come. So let's hope this commercial perspective will drive change, even if common sense doesn't.

Materials and styles: Here's a provocative question: why are we building so few terraced houses? It's a serious point. The fundamental design of a terrace of houses works – and that's why the Victorians built so many of them. The layout is perfect and the structural strength is efficient. And with shared components, fewer materials are required. However, we seem to be obsessed with the need for the modern buyer to have a tiny space in front for their car and a perception of being isolated from their neighbours.

But terraces are one thing; bricks quite another – and one of my real issues is why we are still building houses with bricks. There are much more versatile materials available that would help us build faster and cheaper. They are also better able to deliver the energy performance we so badly need.

For instance, structurally insulated panels, metals and modern plastics all deliver superior insulation properties compared to brick; and they make factory-built prefabrication a reality too. Modern materials are durable and cheap as well as technologically advanced. I can see a future where the outer surfaces of our houses are made from solar PV panels. I just don't understand why we're not striding towards this already.

16: Plug the skills drain

The construction industry makes up a large part of our gross domestic product (GDP). So as it suffers, our country's wealth also suffers. While banks are slowly recovering there will continue to be an uplift in the industry, but it will be short term. Why? The answer is a serious lack of the right skills to continue evolving our housing market.

Indeed, the Royal Institution of Chartered Surveyors (RICS) has announced that house building in the UK is being held up by a lack of bricklayers. Not only are wages increasing to attract talent, which means houses are becoming more expensive to build as a result, but there is also a knock-on effect on the Government's aim of improving infrastructure too.

The organisation's survey reveals that two out of three employers believe that labour shortages are the biggest barrier to the construction industry's growth. There's also an issue with the lack of qualified and experienced quantity surveyors as well, says RICS.

You may not realise it but there is also a massive skills shortage amongst chartered surveyors, architects, solicitors and architectural technicians. And as explained in chapter 7, we're already short of good, qualified builders. All of this adds to the increasing shortage of housing.

People of my generation were lucky, although it's only now that we realise it. Today if you are not especially interested in academic pursuit, it is much harder than it used to be to progress up a parallel skill-based ladder. The government doesn't do enough to encourage and enable companies to take on apprentices or offer jobs to trainees. Many existing schemes are, in my view, laughable.

But the problem actually reaches much further. The skills shortage extends to people involved in the planning process with local authorities cutting back rather than investing in skills. And there is little incentive for property developers to change their own practice, meaning that all the rich opportunities for creating a new housing model based on meeting today's and tomorrow's real housing needs are being missed. Everyone is still chasing a fast buck or being forced to live a cash-strapped hand-to-mouth existence. It is very depressing.

So, there in a nutshell are the big problems with housing and house prices in this country. Not enough new homes are being built; they are not of the right kind and there are too few for first-time buyers, the bedrock of the market but still not supported enough by the government. And previous schemes to address this made very little impact, with only a few fortunate enough to be part of them.

And then there is the question of where new houses are being built; while we continue not to build on green belt land, we are creating communities of people that are forced to commute further and further, increasing levels of pollution while weakening community cohesion. But that, I realise, is a subject for its own entire book...

17: How to negotiate a sale

This is the final chapter in the book and it's an important one because here I will discuss how a Smart Buyer can and should negotiate the sale of a property. This is probably the most important stage in the process of becoming a Smart Buyer and, armed with a surveyor's report, the buyer is in a very good position to negotiate on price and with the builder's estimates for repair costs, the buyer is also able to negotiate on the costs to rectify any problems.

The Smart Buyer should always remember this saying: Condition before price.

This is a simple way to appreciate and realise that the Smart Buyer will need to have a real understanding of how much they can offer on a property because they can't do so without knowing its true condition. This is effectively what someone would do if they were buying a vintage car, for instance, and it's no different to buying a house. This means there is a straightforward recipe for negotiation.

A good starting point is to consider deducting the cost of some repairs because all houses are individuals and this is why you need the help of your qualified and experienced surveyor - otherwise you could lose money! Remember it pays to pay for professional advice.

So, in terms of negotiation I would advise the following:

The Smart Buyer should put in their initial offer. When this initial offer is rejected, they should then go up in the following denominations which are related to the house price; if the house stands at £100,000, for example, you will then increase your offer in lumps of £100, if it's £200,000 then the offer increases by £200 and this formula works for houses worth up to £500,000 when the Smart Buyer negotiates only in chunks of £500. From experience, I believe this is a sound way to negotiate on property prices all the way up to a property worth £900,000 when specialist negotiations will be necessary.

If we appreciate that the average UK house price is nearly £200,000, and, for example, it needs around £8,000 worth of repairs which could be typical and could include border replacements and electrical works. In this instance, the Smart Buyer would go back to the vendor and say you are prepared to offer £192,000. If they then say no, then offer them £192,100. If they say no again, then offer the vendor £192,200.

You will then increase the price and until there comes a point of distortion and acceptance when everybody involved in the negotiations appreciates that the price is not going to go up substantially. Now this is the important bit to remember, I'm a big believer that most people buy houses from their local estate agents and most of these local estate agents are used to negotiating.

Indeed, most estate agents that I know are very capable at negotiations with potential buyers and with good joined-up thinking with buyer, purchaser, surveyor and the estate agent you can come to a deal. This inevitably means that all parties will be discussing the asking price and offering counter-offers to reach a final offer on the property. It helps that the vendor is made aware of the facts and of the necessary repairs to their property to help ensure a quick sale.

In a rising market, the process of negotiating a price can become futile. Prior to the recent recession, there was never much negotiation and it was very much the opposite occurring when people began offering more than other bidders which led to the wonderful term of 'gazumping'. As I will discuss later in this chapter, I do not believe we will return to those days at some point in the near future.

Essentially, we must all appreciate that local estate agents are in business for themselves and have the best interests of their clients at heart and I have found it much easier to deal with a local estate agent much more than with a franchised or online estate agency, for instance. Indeed, some of the local franchises are really good but these are the ones that are run along the lines of a quasi small business.

However, I should also point out that from my own personal and professional experience, there's only one national franchise chain of estate agents I would recommend but, for various legal reasons, I cannot name them in this chapter. I would be, however, willing to speak to those who want to discuss this issue further.

I sincerely believe that a Smart Buyer will encourage joined-up thinking from everyone involved in the selling of a property, from the vendor, estate agents and surveyor as well as themselves, they will instigate a conversation that's realistic and honest at the same time. This will lead to a 'quality circle' and bring about a fair and realistic price for the property for everyone involved.

In times when house prices are falling, then the sky, literally, becomes the limit. The advantage of buying a property from an estate agent and not at auction is that the Smart Buyer is able to do some negotiation because once you buy a property at auction and the hammer falls, that is it. What you get, is what you have bought. These properties really are sold as seen.

Just to wrap up this chapter the following section really could be the frequently asked questions when approaching an estate agent with an offer.

What happens if the estate agent does not pass on my offer?

I must admit that I do not know of any estate agent that would not pass on an offer to their vendors. However, I'm not going to say that the practice does not exist and I have no doubts that many vendors will insist that they will not accept offers lower than a certain amount which the agent must then respect. Indeed, it would be a good thing if we were going to change the way we buy and sell property in England and Wales that the person bidding knew whether there was a 'reserve' price for it - rather like people selling goods on eBay which will have a statement saying 'reserve not met' so the buyer is aware of how low an offer the seller might be willing to accept.

Most estate agents that I know are quite humble and genuine so they have a duty of care to pass on any offer made for a property to their client. Indeed, as a Smart Buyer you could contact the estate agent to put your offer in and you could also put it on a postcard and drop it through the letterbox of the vendor's property.

It's also a good idea when viewing a property to ask for the vendor's email or contact details so that when an offer is made, they are aware of it and how much the offer actually is. It will also help to have the survey done first so the Smart Buyer will have what I term as the 'sea bed' price, which is the lowest amount the property is actually worth. It should also be appreciated that when they make an offer, it's not always the estate agent who rejects it. Some people may believe that because estate agents are working on a commission they will want to crank up the price but if you take of £5,000 from a £200,000 house that's a negligible amount affecting the estate agent's commission.

We should also remember that many estate agents are also increasingly offering fixed price selling fees of £500 or less. So while the vendor may be saving themselves several hundred pounds in fees, the estate agent offering this service will often be undervaluing their property by several thousand pounds in order to gain a quick sale.

Will I be put under pressure?

The entire house buying and selling process in this country is highly pressurised but a Smart Buyer will stand back from the situation to assess properly what the house is worth and make a reasoned offer on it. This may mean that the process itself takes slightly longer because they've gone for the survey first but it does mean that their offer and enthusiasm to buy the house is more real and effective than someone who is essentially bidding blind because they may not know the condition of the property and what repairs may be necessary. You know there is a lot to be said for the house buying system in Scotland ,which is more synchronised than the system found in England and Wales and, hopefully, one day the government may appreciate what the 'Yorkshire Surveyor' is saying to improve the process for everyone involved in buying property.

It should also be appreciated that the person selling the property also wants a buyer who is not going to waste their time with bids that never materialise into an exchange of contracts so while having the survey done first does make the process slightly longer it also underlines the potential buyer's commitment to completing the purchasing process because they have invested money into ensuring that this is the property they really want.

How many times should you view a property?

There's no set answer for this but a Smart Buyer will inspect the property more than once, and preferably one of these visits will be with a qualified surveyor. There has been research published which reveals that the more times a potential buyer visits a property not only leads to a sale but also to a sale with a lower asking price. I'm inclined to believe this from my own experiences and this also leads me onto another growing trend....

Can I try before I buy?

There is an interesting trend developing which sees people trying property for size before actually buying it. From what I've seen, those who do live in the property for a day or two really do commit to buying it because they essentially fall in love with it and know that it is right for them and their needs. I have met at least half a dozen buyers who have been to stay in a property on a Friday and Saturday night. Indeed, I spoke to a really nice couple recently who said that when they tried out the property they did want to leave and it was ideal for them. I appreciate that this idea has taken off in America but it does appear to be coming here as well and, for many people, it looks like a great idea to consider.

Personally, I think it also gives time for the buyer to think about what concerns them and this may be the point when they discover that their next door neighbour is the drummer in a heavy rock band who plays his drums at 3am every day, for instance!

During the research for this book I've spoken to real estate agents from many countries, including the United States as well as Australian estate agents and they are all interested in what we do. The best conversation I've had recently is with an estate agent from South Africa and they were gobsmacked about the pressure that buyers and sellers are under in the UK and it appears that most other countries have a more relaxed approach to house selling and we need to follow in their footsteps to slow down our process because we will, in the long run, sell more homes. That's because a more relaxed and less time-intensive process will enable the problems to be ironed out and the pipeline to run more smoothly.

By taking more time, the vendor and the buyer will appreciate what problems there are with a property and this is what I find when I spend time speaking with estate agents about a particular report because they understand what I am trying to say and what the potential impact could be on the buyer. Indeed, this probably

193

explains why so many estate agents collaborate with us and us with them because we explain what we are trying to do and I find that once you explain things to people, it takes away the fear factor.

When should I walk away?

A smart buyer should never be afraid to walk away from the deal that is not in their best interests and they should also appreciate when is the best time to walk away. There are hundreds of reasons why someone would walk away from a deal which range from having a lifestyle change, sometimes getting cold feet or even getting divorced. I also believe that the pressure of the system also affects people and how they make a decision with many people being rushed into buying a property that either has problems or isn't really for them.

Knowing when to walk away from the deal depends largely on the buyer's lifestyle. For instance, if you are buying an 1860s cottage and the surveyor's report paints a rather grim outlook about all the repairs it needs which means the potential buyer then needs to consider whether they have enough cash to carry out the repairs and secondly whether they have the time for the repairs to be carried out effectively.

More importantly, the potential buyer also needs to understand that they have the patience and state of mind to carry out the repairs because they will, inevitably, become a stressful and costly exercise to undertake. Regardless of a smart buyer's lifestyle changes, they must always enter the process of property buying with their eyes wide open; they must be certain from the very beginning that they want to buy a particular property.

There's also the issue that some properties may have strings attached. For instance, there are some properties I've been involved with where the land is actually leased to another company so a Smart Buyer may find that their back garden is theirs under lease because it's owned by another organisation.

It's not surprising really that this situation would put many potential buyers off whereas others will have been put off after visiting the property on a Friday night or gone back at a different time and then realised that there are dozens of dustbin lorries passing from the property every morning and no one's mentioned it previously.

This means I cannot put my finger on one single reason as to why a Smart Buyer should walk away from buying a property that they want; it's all down to individual circumstances and discovering more about the property and the area in which it stands. However, it's also important to appreciate that if you do walk away from a deal that you'll learn something from the experience and you can then utilise the experience for the next property you want to buy. I should also point out that you should not let the situation of circumstances that led to the breakdown of one sale dictate the process and your appreciation of the next property sale.

This is also a good point to remind readers that they should never view their potential property purchase as being theirs to actually live in, regardless of how they can see how great their life will be in it. This is an issue that Peter Gibson, a property solicitor, raises in appendix 1 and is perfectly correct in what he says that until the contracts are exchanged, the property is not yours.

Again, I should also highlight that we work with lots of local solicitors and the chances are that at some point in the past they have dealt with the sale or purchasing of a particular property and their own experience of it may bring fresh advice or opinion on the purchase.

The smart buyer is better informed by getting all of their facts together and will then use the property professional as well as using people who know and care about their own job and who care about you as a property buyer and the vendor which brings us back to local knowledge.

Successful property buying really is about being a Smart Buyer and utilising local knowledge and it's also down to independence. The key thing that every buyer should appreciate is that before they make an offer they need to find out what they are buying and it's crucial that they get a survey first before putting an offer in. And as we stated in a previous chapter, the Smart Buyer is in charge of the process and they should not be dictated to or forced into making a decision or an offer they are not sure about being confident of completing.

So what does the future hold for the UK's property market?

Before signing off, I thought I would give a bold prediction for the UK's property market because so many people ask me on a regular basis. To me, the property market is a ticking time bomb, in fact it's a nuclear bomb! When this bomb explodes, it will undoubtedly annihilate the British economy and it's now just a matter of when. What set the fuse for this ticking time bomb?

Well, the simple answer is the lack of first-time buyers in the market and the lack of Government intervention to allow cheap mortgages and we are now living in a society where young people, generally our first-time buyers, are having to rent property that costs them more than a mortgage would cost. There's no doubt that the lack of first-time buyers will lead to a massive drought in the housing market and I am predicting that it could be around 2025, or slightly after, and if there has been no Government intervention and no first-time buyers any more then house prices will start to fall and the housing market will rapidly deflate; properties will still sell but it will be a much slower process and, in essence, without first-time buyers which are the lifeblood of the housing market and always have been - which we seem to have forgotten - then the UK's housing market will become virtually extinct.

Jon's most important tip for Smart Buyers everywhere:

The most important piece of advice I have saved until the very last

As a Smart Buyer you should never lose sight of the fact that you are in charge – not the estate agent or the solicitor or the mortgage lender.

This is YOUR home and YOUR money so refuse to be railroaded into making a decision because if it is the wrong one then it is you that will have to pay the price for it.

A final word (on behalf of small British businesses...)

This book has been written to raise awareness of, and propose solutions for, the problems that plague today's buyers and sellers of houses in the UK. They are archaic problems that slow everything down, including the national economy. However, this is itself a symptom of a wider problem that affects so many people across the country – an establishment blindness in acknowledging an unacceptable status quo and an inertia in doing anything about it.

Look, we live in a country where beyond the privileged zone within the M25, roads can be closed off by cones with no roadworks taking place, and where the moment you venture into more rural areas you must expect inferior mobile phone connectivity and slower broadband (if any at all). These are symptomatic problems that a) should not be down to a London-centric postcode lottery and b) could be resolved within one year if the will were there.

But for as long as they continue it is the small businesses around the country that really take the battering; and a great many of those are represented here in this book in the form of local estate agents, solicitors and surveyors. Small businesses work tirelessly and innovatively to thrive in the UK economy but are hampered by government inertia and bias *and* by the extortionate rates of corporation tax and VAT charged by HMRC.

There is no logic whatsoever in continuing to jeopardise small businesses with unfair corporation tax; the economy needs us to survive, so why will the government refuse to introduce reduced tax bands based on size of turnover? This is what small businesses have asked for, loudly and clearly. But no one appears to be listening.

Small businesses are bullied; it is as simple as that. It is time that something acted as a catalyst to end the policies that sustains this. I don't for a moment expect this book to achieve that, but it may help take a few small steps further towards the change we all need and ask for.

Appendix 1: Why Smart Home Buyers and sellers should use professionals

By Peter Gibson,

Managing Director of Coles Solicitors.

As a property solicitor I would urge everyone who wants to be a smart home buyer or seller to use professionals. This way they will avoid potential headaches and expensive costs if the legal work is not done effectively. I realise that surveyor's and solicitor's fees can be expensive and those on a budget might be tempted to cut costs. But I would advise you against this action.

HOW IT LOOKS FROM MY PERSPECTIVE

The author is absolutely right when he recommends that smart home buyers should use local professionals such as solicitors, surveyors and estate agents because there are idiosyncrasies to every area that only these experts will know of. This is particularly true when you are dealing with legal matters relating to property.

A local law firm may have dealt with a particular property multiple times and they can then go back and look at their previous records, previous searches and know about the previous ownership of land. This could be crucial and I can think of at least half a dozen properties that we, as a company, have dealt with advantageously given our local experience.

For instance, there's a property on the edge of one town that has been bought and sold six times in the last seven years and we have either acted for the buyer or the seller on each of those transactions. I mention this because when it was sold seven years ago, there were problems with the Land Registry as some parts of the land had not been properly registered. But, using our own internal knowledge and past records, we were able to piece together an accurate picture that made the process of selling the property so much easier.

Knowledge of the local area can be vital too. A remote agent or solicitor may not be aware that an area has had an awful lot of gypsum mined in it in the past, causing sink holes and risks to property in the area. And some areas (like Scarborough with its freehold flats) have very unusual aspects to their housing markets with particular legal idiosyncrasies for dealing with that issue.

There are a whole range of reasons why house buyers and sellers should use local professionals; they not only bring experience and expertise but also the convenience of being able to pop into their offices whenever necessary. Sometimes it's important to see someone you are dealing with face-to-face and that's not always the case if your solicitor is sat hundreds of miles away.

So, what happens when your mortgage lender nominates a professional for you to use? These are panel firms appointed by mortgage lenders, and whilst I cannot pick on any one firm and name them, my advice is to be very wary of using them. Generally speaking, these panel firms have been bargained with and their fees negotiated down to the lowest, cheapest common denominator by the bank concerned to ensure that every ounce of profit is screwed out of the transaction in favour of the bank itself.

Those costs and savings have to be met somewhere, for example by not using qualified experienced professionals. Another is to provide a less professional service and not to answer calls from clients and for the legal firm to 'streamline' the service which means the client will never get to speak with the same person twice.

This means the legal firm will commoditise the process so one person will deal with the initial part, and then pass the transaction onto a colleague who will then deal with the next stage and the transaction is passed along what is effectively a conveyor belt with an absence of consistent or reliable advice.

It is widely acknowledged within the legal sector that the level of service provided by these firms is, generally, poor. On more than one occasion we have had to unpick the work done by one of these panel-appointed 'conveyancing factories' because it appears they do not know what they are doing. For instance, there may be a technical error in the legal title and there may be some problems with the legal aspects of the property that have generated an administrative mess; these require someone with some intelligence, education, background knowledge and legal expertise to resolve.

When dealing with some of these big 'factories', there may be just one qualified solicitor overseeing the work of perhaps 10 or even up to 50 people who are not qualified and not experienced. The firm undertaking this work is complying from a regulatory point of view but the question must be asked whether they are providing a quality service.

One thing you will rarely be told is that there is no legal requirement for you to appoint a solicitor for your conveyancing. You can do it yourself if you want. It will be difficult but it will not be impossible. Alternatively, you can also instruct a licensed conveyancer to do the work; they are specialists in this field and while they are not regulated by the SRA (the Solicitors Regulation Authority) they are still a regulated service so there are no problems when dealing with them.

Jon is absolutely right to draw your attention to the difference between a valuation and a proper survey. My firm's website has a free download which explains the house buying process for buyers and sellers alike and within it we stress the importance of having a thorough survey done of the property.

But, frankly, anyone who has seen a valuation report will realise that they are mostly not worth the paper they are written on. It should be highlighted that the mortgage lender happily accepting a valuation is reliant upon the fact that solicitors, as well as surveyors and valuers, have got professional indemnity insurance.

During the last recession when mortgage repossessions went up, the mortgage lender took the keys back and put the property through an auction to sell at a rock bottom price to reclaim some of their money. If this process left them short of money, they would initially go out after the surveyor and then, secondly, they would go after the solicitor to make up the difference.

It's for this reason that solicitors pay the heaviest premiums for professional indemnity insurance of any of the professions in this country – more than doctors, dentists, architects and surveyors; it is a phenomenal expense.

Another issue we highlight in our download is not to 'jump the gun' ahead of the completion and exchange date. Compared to Scotland, the single biggest problem we have in this country is that nothing is binding from a legal point of view until the exchange of contracts has happened. That is generally three or four-weeks down the line from the buyer's offer being accepted by the sellers; and in the meantime, anything could happen.

For instance, something in the survey or the solicitor's searches may lead the buyer to withdraw from the sale. In addition, the buyer's financial situation may change and they no longer can afford to buy the property or they no longer qualify for the mortgage criteria; there's a whole panoply of things that could go wrong. So until the exchange of contracts happens there is no guarantee whatsoever that you will legally get that property.

Smart house buying means being ruled by your head, not your heart. It's easy to say but difficult in the moment. Let's be honest, if you are buyer of a property and you make an offer then you have, in your own mind, effectively moved into the property. You have already decided where you are putting the furniture, what colour you are going to paint the living room and you can see yourself in that beautiful roll-top bath.

I know what it's like and I've done it myself; and in your mind as the buyer your mortgage lender, your financial adviser, the surveyor, and, worst of all, your solicitor are all standing in the way of your moving into your house. The crucial thing is to remember that it is not yet your house.

I also warn house buyers not to expect the keys to their new property at 9am on completion day. Many try to insist that they get the keys at this time, but there are still various transactions to complete on the day of completion. This means that they will generally not get the keys until 2pm when the seller's solicitors confirms receipt of the money in their account.

And should the money not arrive with the solicitors by 2pm you will then, legally, be deemed to have completed on the next following working day. Obviously, through experience there is a bit of give and take and a practical approach is used to ensure that the deadline is met with and the buyer gets the keys.

On the other hand, in many cases the seller has had the removals van at their property at 8am and by 10am they have an empty property; and if the money has already arrived in the seller's bank account there's no reason why they can't release the keys to the buyer. I have had many instances of the keys being handed into the estate agents on the day before completion and the buyer has moved into rented accommodation or emigrated.

Generally speaking, the only things that could go wrong on completion date is for there to be a glitch in the banking system; the CHAPS system could go down, but there's nothing we can do because this is out of our hands.

ADVICE FOR BECOMING A SMARTER BUYER AND SELLER

My first piece of advice for anyone wanting to be a smarter property buyer is to get your mortgage agreed in principle before you even begin looking for a property. It's also important that you know your financial limits and do further research as to which solicitors you should use; research online and read reviews if necessary.

It's also important to shop around before engaging the services of a professional. Although this service can be expensive I would advise not to simply choose the cheapest service being offered. Essentially, I believe in the old adage that if you buy cheap, you will buy twice. It could also pay dividends to engage in a professional who is operating locally.

Word-of-mouth recommendations are important, particularly from family and friends, but I would be wary of an estate agent making a recommendation for a professional's services. That's not to say you should not listen to them because small, independent local estate agents will generally know who is good locally and who works hard with them. However, everyone should be smart and appreciate that there may be a financial incentive for one professional to recommend the services of another.

For anyone who thinks this may be difficult to find out they should be aware that if the estate agent and solicitor are complying fully with the rules then this referral fee will be declared in the terms and conditions of the solicitor. If it is not, either the solicitor or the estate agent or both are not complying with their necessary regulations.

I am not knocking the services of the solicitor who has been recommended on the basis of a referral fee. It does not mean that the solicitor's services will be shoddy or slapdash; it is simply another route to market that solicitor's services in order to generate business. It is important to appreciate too that this way of generating work is not that much different from firms advertising on Google and many people don't realise when they click on a link that they are clicking on an advert.

From speaking with Jon about his book, one of the issues I strongly agree about is the problem of people disputing how much professional fees cost. We now live in a world where we will go out and queue for several hours outside the Apple shop to pay £600 or £700 for a telephone.

But when it comes to buying professional services such as a surveys or legal help, we do not appear as a society to value these in the way that we should. We need to move away from thinking of professional help as a cost or expense and see it for what it is – peace of mind.

People need to appreciate that when they engage a solicitor to help them buy a property they are using their expertise in helping to avoid a potential purchase that's got pitfalls and problems. The buyer needs the peace of mind that they have the full legal title to the property, that everything is in good working order and is not about to collapse or be repossessed, and that no one is about to build a motorway alongside it.

For most people, a house is the most important and expensive purchase they will make in their lifetime and they need to do this in an informed and educated way. The vast majority of homebuyers do not have the information or education that solicitors and surveyors have; and they should remember that professional fees represent the same overheads as any other business as well as the reliable expertise you need.

To me, that is a price worth paying as it will help avoid the potential expensive problems that come from not doing the legal side properly or effectively when buying or selling property.

Peter Gibson has been a qualified solicitor for 15 years and has owned Coles Solicitors for the last 10 years. His firm is at coles-law.co.uk.

How to be a smarter house buyer

Appendix 2: The national and global economies

Why smart home buyers and sellers MUST pay attention to the economy

By Luke Charters-Reid

A smart buyer needs to be aware of signals that suggest impending change in the national and global economies. Whilst there is very little that buyers (and sellers) can do in response to these macroeconomic changes, monitoring them can help determine exactly when to enter the market, how to buy and sell for the best price, how to get government help where applicable and even where to buy their house.

HOW TO BE SMART ABOUT INTEREST RATE HIKES

Why should a buyer in Warrington be concerned about the interest rate decisions being made by the US Federal Reserve?

The era of historically low interest rates is inevitably going to come to an end in the near future. At the time of writing, bank interest rates look likely to begin increasing towards the end of the 2016/7 financial year after a record static low level. Most buyers understand that this will increase the interest on any given mortgage. However, the *smart buyer* will keep a keen eye on global financial activity in order to get a 'heads-up' that can help them to plan their purchasing decisions wisely.

One place to be looking is the US. The Bank of England has typically followed the US Federal Reserve in raising interest rates – although this is not always the case. Given that low Bank of England base rates have recently been attributable to low demand in the economy, an increase in interest rates acts as a reasonable hint to buyers and sellers that demand is picking up in the economy. The caveat is that low-oil prices are leading to what is known as 'cost-push' deflationary pressures, which may delay an increase in the base rate, despite demand picking up in the domestic economy.

What impact will an interest rate rise have on home buyers (and sellers)?

For the *smart buyer* it means deciding whether to opt for a lower-priced property than they may have considered just a few months earlier. However, more generally there is the worry that rising interest rates will price even more people out of the property market altogether, something which I think is genuinely being taken seriously by policymakers across the country.

Buyers should definitely look to the government's new Help to Buy loan scheme as a bulwark against forthcoming rate increases. For instance, the government will offer loans of up to 40% of a new build property value for first time buyers, meaning that they have to rely less on mortgages (for example putting in their own 5% deposit and then only needing a 55% mortgage).

In terms of that 5% deposit, there is another useful device for first time buyers wishing to be smart – the 'Help to Buy ISA'. This is an account where you can save around £200 per month on which you receive around 4% interest *and* a 25% bonus on all monies saved when you close the account and use it towards a deposit. With the bonus limited to a maximum of £3,000 the total sum you can save is relatively small, but still useful as part of a broader ambition to save for a first home.

So, with interest rates likely to rise, what type of mortgage should you go for? Clearly, buyers taking out a base-rate interest-tracking mortgage will feel the effects of rising interest most starkly. However, taking out a fixed-term mortgage may not be the better option that many buyers assume. Banks plan for this and a variety of other factors when setting mortgage rates, making them hard to beat whichever product you opt for.

As the book's author has quite rightly stressed, it is highly advisable that people consult an independent financial advisor (IFA) about the variety of products available. In addition to this, a useful tip is that the incentives for switching bank accounts (and the ease of so doing) are also becoming an increasingly common feature in the mortgage market. So a *smart buyer* will shop around and look at some of the new emerging players in the banking sector, as well as building societies, which are able to specialise in mortgaging provision; and smart owners will routinely review mortgage deals from other lenders.

Property Price Bubbles

When there is a rapid increase in demand for property in a given area without sufficient construction of new homes it leads to a bubble in property prices. Prices rise and remain high until change in demand, or volatility and speculation in the market, cause the bubble to burst.

Why should a seller in Cardiff be bothered about the state of the Shanghai stock exchange? The answer: it gives a good indication of the steadiness (or volatility) in the global market, the effects of which trickle all the way back to Cardiff.

As a general rule, if a recession is looming it makes sense to sell now before property values fall – or, if buying, to delay until they do. Realistically, of course, most people don't have this flexibility, but they can still benefit a little by watching out for any property price bubbles that are likely to burst. And while a stock market bubble does not necessarily mean an imminent property price bubble, they are most probably linked.

A bubble is a temporary state, and bubbles can either deflate or burst very suddenly. Bubbles deflate rapidly if there is a considerable decrease in the demand in the property sector, or in the economy more generally as in a recession. However, if there is considerable overheating in the economy, such as was the case in the late 1980s where there was a Japanese asset price bubble, it can lead to a sudden burst in the property bubble. Both deflations and bursts can be influenced by oil prices, exposure to the Chinese economy, and other factors such as another banking crisis.

The areas most susceptible to price bubbles are typically those in proximity to, or situated within, a capital city. Hence the wider area of the South East is particularly vulnerable. So, the smart buyer in this part of the country needs to be very conscious of any premium that they are paying for the location in addition to the property's underlying value. Why? Because this is the component most likely to reduce with the popping of a bubble. When the bubble bursts – and unfortunately this has been an inevitability in the past – all those who own property are impacted. However, the timing is key.

Imagine a bubble occurs in 2025, one year after you bought a charming terraced house just outside the centre of York in 2024. If you choose not to sell it during the bubble then the value will ultimately recede back to its pre-bubble level, so you are unaffected. However, let's say that by 2025 you have some spare cash and want to speculate in another property. You will make the best profit by buying during the bubble's burst, at the bottom of the market, and then selling high during the price recovery period. The flipside of this is the trap many people find themselves in, negative equity, where they bought at the top of the market and then find they have borrowed more than the readjusted price after the bubble bursts.

What this all means for the smart buyer is that you need to factor in the potential for bubbles, and possibly be ready to live slightly further away from your preferred area to avoid the negative impact of a property bubble.

There is currently a big debate about what most influences our spending habits. Going back to the 1950s, the debate considers the microeconomics literature that dates back to the 1950s and the proposition made by MIT economist Franco Modigliani. He proposed the 'life-cycle model' in which we our spending and consumption is driven more by our average income than our actual wealth. This is all well and good but the counter-argument is that, as people see their property value massively increasing, they feel much richer and then, in turn, borrow even more against their property.

If true, this increases their vulnerability to property bubbles (and interest rate hikes), meaning that the effects are likely to be greater, with a higher chance that they end up in the dystopia of negative equity. [For those interested, this essentially the neo-Keynesian view of debt in the economy]

However, returning to current times, I don't actually see another property bubble occurring any time soon. This is primarily for two reasons:

Firstly, London prices have been stalling in recent quarters; and, secondly, there is an average period of around 15 years between each property bubble.

What matters more to the smart buyer is not an academic debate but the fact that their home is an investment, one of the biggest investments they are ever likely to make.

Of course, most home buyers are paying for lifestyle stability, not profit, but even so were they to be offered the alternative of investing hundreds of thousands of pounds on the stock market in safe assets, they may find paradoxically that buying a house is not the more profitable option.

That is why for a property investor, higher returns (with greater risk) look more likely in city locations, while for a family buying a home, villages and towns on the outskirts of cities look like a more stable and secure investment.

Other Things To Look Out For

- In April 2016, Mr Osborne, the Chancellor, will add an extra 3% to stamp duty on all buy to let purchases. In my mind, there seems to be a general regulatory trend towards cooling down the buy to let market. This means that the smart buyer in this area will undoubtedly need to keep up to date with announcements from the Chancellor in the budget and autumn statements.

- Buyers should also be aware of the local regulatory environment as local councils are using recently acquired powers to make it harder for houses to be turned into student houses. This means that in some university towns, Oxford being a case in point, buy to let acquisitions are becoming more risky. They are also becoming less profitable as landlord licencing fees are on the rise.

• Changes to the 'shadow banking system': I think there is a genuine concern among economists that the next financial crisis will be one triggered by some sort of failure in the shadow banking system, especially as regulators have to play catch-up with respect to emerging financial institutions.

As a final twin plea – my first big shout out to policymakers is that we really need to end stamp duty for first time buyers; and my second is to increase some of the limits on first time buyers' schemes while prices continue to rise rapidly.

Luke Charters-Reid is reading Philosophy, Politics, and Economics at the University of Oxford. He has previously interned at the Bank of England.